IMAGES
*of America*

# RUIDOSO AND
# RUIDOSO DOWNS

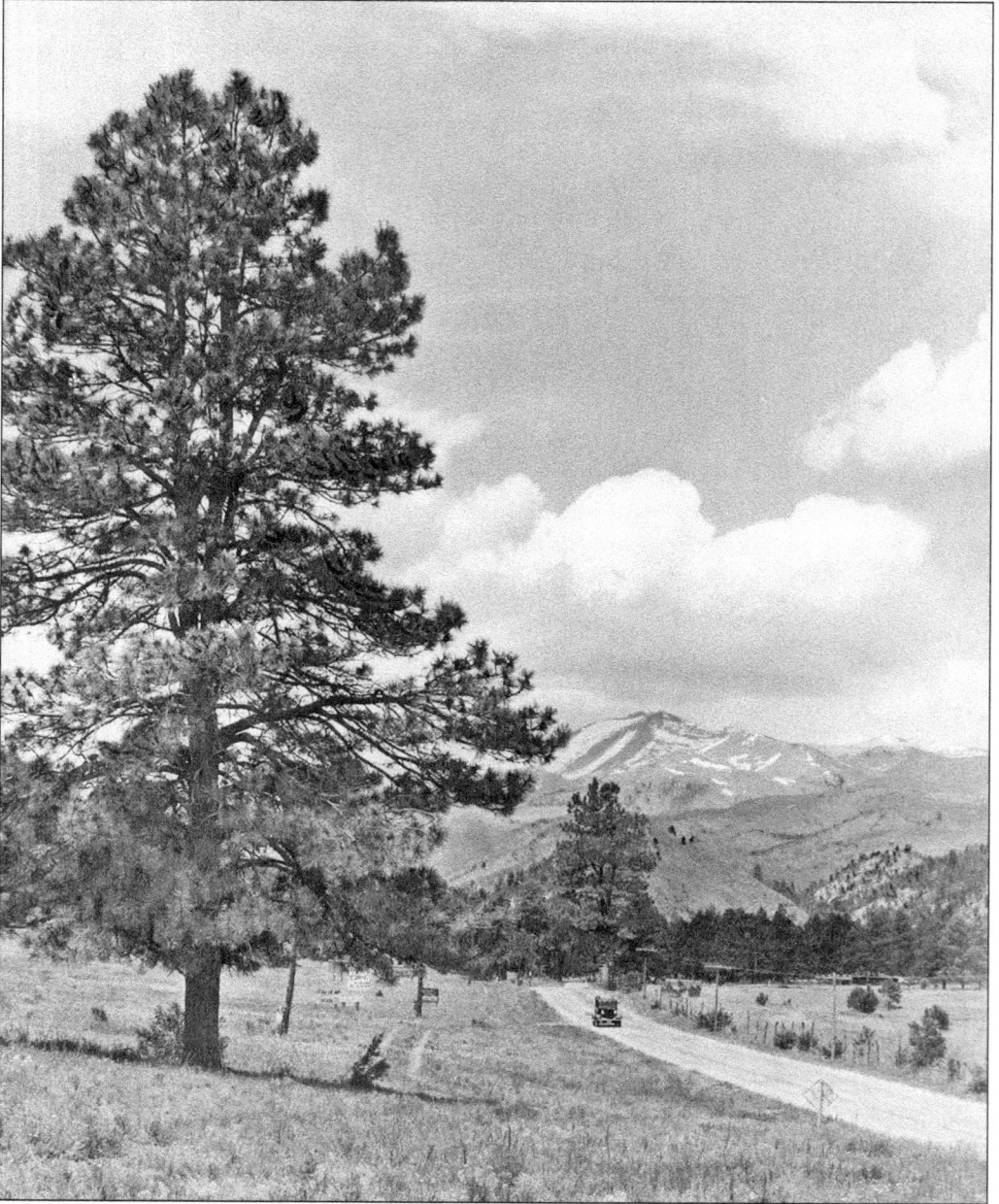

Early travelers often navigated by the peak of Sierra Blanca, also known as "Old Baldy." In fact, author Frank Mangan remembered family trips from El Paso in the 1930s: "We'd just slowly wind around the sand hills, following the railroad track, and all the time Sierra Blanca would be right there in front of us." (Courtesy of Elsie Williams.)

ON THE COVER: In 1948, Midtown Ruidoso was filled with people ready to forget their troubles and the war and just have a good time. The town's Main Road was lined with dance halls, bars, and gambling establishments. At Hollywood Park (later Ruidoso Downs Race Track), big money was bet on whose horse was the fastest. Less than a mile away, one could find solitude and natural beauty in the forested slopes and river canyons. (Courtesy of Herb Brunell.)

IMAGES
*of America*

# RUIDOSO AND
# RUIDOSO DOWNS

Lyn Kidder and Herb Brunell

ARCADIA
PUBLISHING

Copyright © 2009 by Lyn Kidder and Herb Brunell
ISBN 978-1-5316-4632-5

Published by Arcadia Publishing
Charleston, South Carolina


Library of Congress Control Number: 2008938757

For all general information contact Arcadia Publishing at:
Telephone 843-853-2070
Fax 843-853-0044
E-mail sales@arcadiapublishing.com
For customer service and orders:
Toll-Free 1-888-313-2665

Visit us on the Internet at www.arcadiapublishing.com

*To everyone who ever had a good time in Ruidoso*

# CONTENTS

# ACKNOWLEDGMENTS

We would like to thank the following organizations for their help with this book: the Hubbard Museum of the American West, the Hurd Gallery, the Ruidoso Public Library, the *Ruidoso News*, the Hubbard Foundation, the Spencer Theater, the Smokey Bear Museum, New Mexico State University Archives and Special Collections, MTD Radio, the Ruidoso Downs Race Track, and the Ruidoso Regional Council for the Arts.

We would also like to thank the following individuals for taking time to pull out dusty old books, sort through old photographs, remember just who, what, when, and where about the photographs, and answer all our questions: the Barajas family, Betty Bennett, Richard Bryant, Eleanor Bonnell, Terry and Kemp Christian, Delana Clements, Mickey Cochran, Mary Guck Crenshaw, Lloyd Davis, Robyn Fleenor, Nyela Hand, Wayne Joyce, Jodie Keyes, Herb Marsh, Bill McCarty, Roy Parker, Dave Parks, Dr. Alden Ritch, Betsy Seiler, John and Dixie Sigler, Sharon Stewart, Joetyne Wright, and Ty Wyant.

# INTRODUCTION

It all began with the mountain.

Above the surrounding desert, Sierra Blanca's 12,000-foot peak rises like a mirage. Approximately 30 million years ago, subterranean volcanic activity pushed up an enormous mountain, so large that the mountain of today is only the molten rock that slowly cooled inside the volcano. It is the southernmost mountain in the United States with an elevation that supports alpine vegetation. In fact, the terrain from the Tularosa Basin to the summit—a distance of some 50 miles—encompasses six life zones, from lower Sonoran desert to arctic alpine.

Because of its height and exposed position, storms build on its slopes. "Sierra Blanca," Spanish for "white mountain," refers to the snow that caps it during part of the year; its nickname "Old Baldy" refers to its rounded, treeless summit. On the eastern side of the mountain, lush forests of Douglas fir, aspen, and ponderosa pine grow among a network of streams that eventually join the Rio Ruidoso. The western slope is steeper, more rugged, and much drier.

There is evidence that Native Americans were drawn to its heights. Between 900 and 1400 AD, the Jornada Mogollon people created more than 21,000 petroglyphs at Three Rivers, the western base of the mountain. More recently, the Mescalero Apache consider Sierra Blanca—Dzil gais' ání or "mountain with snow on top" in Apache—to be the home of their protectors, the Mountain Gods.

The location of early settlements in Lincoln County was based on mineral wealth, military importance, and arable land rather than scenic beauty. The Hispanic farmers who settled along the Rio Bonito in what was first New Spain and later Mexico found a market for their hay, beef, and grain at Fort Stanton, the U.S. Army post established in 1855 to provide protection from Apache raids. In 1869, Lincoln County was created, and the region's largest community, Las Placitas del Rio Bonito, was renamed "Lincoln."

About the same time, former soldier Paul Dowlin and his brother Will built an adobe mill on the bank of the Rio Ruidoso, and a small community grew up around it.

The Lincoln County War—a struggle for political and economic domination of the region and the state—is itself the subject of many books. The young outlaw known as Billy the Kid is the best-known character of the conflict, and the forests along the Ruidoso certainly provided hiding places for members of both factions.

When some measure of public safety was established, a few summer visitors ventured up. Although the mountain is tantalizingly visible for up to 100 miles in nearly every direction, it was inaccessible to all but the most determined, being a three-day journey by wagon from Roswell, only 90 miles away, and at least four weary days from El Paso.

By 1907, a primitive road had been graded from Alamogordo to Roswell. Visitors returning home with stories of cool forests and swift mountain streams encouraged more visitors to make the journey. The town of Ruidoso, established in 1891, began to have a few more permanent residents, notably the Wingfield family. Most of the land belonged to James Cree, a wealthy Scotsman who invested in land and cattle in the 1880s, so most early visitors simply camped along the riverbanks. In 1915, a group of people convinced James Cree's descendants to lease some land in what became known as Upper Canyon, and the first summer cabins were built.

During the Great Depression, nearly one-third of New Mexicans were unemployed, but Ruidoso continued to grow. The town's reputation as a place to have a good time expanded to include gambling in its many bars, restaurants, and stores. The town incorporated in 1945, with a reported 40¢ in the treasury and one paid employee. During the first year, the town supported itself on liquor taxes, garbage collection fees, and police court fines.

During World War II, the nearby military facilities—Walker Air Force Base in Roswell, Fort Bliss in El Paso, and White Sands Proving Ground in Alamogordo—provided a steady stream of servicemen. When gas rationing ended, Americans hit the highways and explored the United States—including Ruidoso.

The town's chamber of commerce was officially organized in 1944 and embarked on an enthusiastic promotion of the town, hosting celebrities and giving a week's stay to a winner of the popular radio and television show *Queen for a Day*. At the end of the Los Angeles resident's stay, she was asked what she thought of the town. "We'd like to roll it up and take it with us," she replied, and the town loved it.

Artists discovered the area and opened their studios for summer art classes. A few miles down the river, near a community named Hollywood, people informally gathered to see just whose horse was faster. A more or less official racetrack called Hollywood Park opened in 1945. New owners continued to improve and expand the track, which was renamed Ruidoso Downs in 1958. The racetrack is home to the All American Futurity, the world's richest quarter horse race, with an annual purse of more than $1 million.

Although residents and some early visitors enjoyed winter sports, the area remained primarily a summer resort. The local saying was that one could "shoot a cannon down Main Road after Labor Day and not hit anyone." A small ski area opened at the end of Cedar Creek in 1938, with locals selling lift tickets and sandwiches and operating the gasoline-powered rope tow. In 1960, negotiations with the U.S. Forest Service led to permission to build a ski area on Sierra Blanca.

More than a century has passed since the first visitors made the difficult trip up the mountain. Today the journey is smoother and faster, but visitors still come for the same reasons. They come to hike, fish, and camp in a setting of unspoiled natural beauty. They come for the excitement of horse racing and casino gambling. And they come to simply sit on the porch and listen to the wind in the pines or—in the early morning hours when traffic is light—to the noisy waters of the Rio Ruidoso.

# One

# EARLY DAYS

The Sacramento Mountains were only a small part of the vast territory that the Mescalero Apaches called home. The Spaniards called it "Apacheria," and it extended from Texas to California and from Colorado to Mexico. The nomadic Apaches, naturally, spent winters in the warmer desert areas at lower elevation and summers in the mountains. The Mescalero Apaches took their name from the mescal plant, a desert agave with an edible root. The harshness of the land made the livestock of the new settlers especially tempting to the Apaches, and the U.S. Army was brought in to subdue them.

Fort Stanton, established in 1855, provided economic opportunity to area farmers and ranchers in the form of government contracts for beef, grain, and (probably at the request of Irish-American soldiers) potatoes. After the tragically failed attempt to relocate the Mescalero Apaches to Bosque Redondo, they were allowed to return to the Sacramento Mountains in 1873. The Indian Agency created even more demand for beef and grain.

Gold was discovered 40 miles north of Ruidoso in 1879, and the town of White Oaks boomed during the next 20 years with a newspaper, bank, opera house, saloons, and a two-story brick schoolhouse. An estimated $3 million in gold and silver were mined in the next 25 years. Other mining communities like Nogal and Bonito City, established in 1908, sprang up in the same area. Farmers and ranchers settled near communities like Angus and Alto, which boasted a school, post office, two stores, and two sawmills by the end of the 19th century. Newspapers commented on the fertile soil and abundant water and reported on promising harvests, including a story in 1919 about a 9.5-pound turnip.

Although Ruidoso itself had a small population, the cool mountain climate attracted parties of campers. An article in the *El Paso Times* in 1889 noted, "There must be extraordinary charms of some sort to lead women and children to brave hardship of a tedious overland trip of 150 miles. Certain it is that the Ruidoso has already won rank as the most popular resort for camping out in all the country for 200 miles about El Paso, a grassy mountain valley surmounted by a dense forest in which weary mortals from the city may hide themselves for a few weeks of rest and refreshment." It went on to predict, "Before many years, summer hotels will abound in the locality."

In 1873, the Mescalero Apache Reservation was moved from Fort Stanton to an area south of Ruidoso in part to avoid the corrupt practices of the J. J. Dolan Company. In a letter to his mother in 1879, 2nd Lt. Walter Finley, stationed at Fort Stanton, wrote, "It is the old story, unjust treatment of the Indians by the Govt., treaties broken, promises violated and the Indians moved from one reservation to another against their will, until finally they break out and go on the war path and the Army is called in to kill them. It is hard to fight against and shoot down men when you know they are in the right and are really doing what our fathers did in the Revolution, fighting for their country." (Both courtesy of the late Carmon Phillips.)

Fort Stanton was established in 1855 to protect settlers from Apache raids. During the Civil War, the retreating Union troops set fire to the fort as Confederate troops approached. A sudden summer thunderstorm put out the fire, but the adobe ruin stood vacant for two years. During its years as a fort, companies of African American "Buffalo soldiers" were stationed there, as well as a young soldier who would later become Gen. John "Blackjack" Pershing. The troops on parade in 1885 (below) wear plumed helmets similar to the Prussian army. In 1898, the fort became a U.S. Marine hospital for patients with tuberculosis. The white tents housing the invalids are visible in the photograph above. In 1953, it was transferred to the State of New Mexico. (Above courtesy of New Mexico State University Library Archives and Special Collections; below courtesy of Eleanor Bonnell.)

In 1868, former soldier Paul Dowlin and his brother Will became Ruidoso's first residents when they built an adobe mill on the riverbank. The first mill was soon destroyed by flood, and they rebuilt on higher ground. A 3-mile wooden flume brought water from the river to turn the mill wheel from a point that became known as Flume Canyon. (Courtesy of Herb Brunell.)

P-18 THE OLD MILL – RUIDOSO, NEW MEXICO.

S.W. Post Card Co.
Albuquerque

The little community officially became Ruidoso in 1891, and the Lesnetts operated its post office in the mill until 1904. The mill served as a stopping place for travelers between Roswell, El Paso, Fort Stanton, and the Indian Agency at Mescalero. It was a social center for soldiers from Fort Stanton and employees of the Indian Agency. (Courtesy of Herb Brunell.)

In 1877, Annie Lesnett journeyed from Chicago to join her husband, Frank, who had recently become part owner of Paul Dowlin's mill. They arrived in Ruidoso the day after Dowlin was killed by a disgruntled employee. In spite of this inauspicious beginning, the Lesnetts raised their family in the mill. Annie later recounted visits by Billy the Kid, who washed dishes and minded the baby. (Courtesy of the late Carmon Phillips.)

The mill was said to be neutral territory during the Lincoln County War, although Annie Lesnett claimed to have hidden Billy the Kid in an empty flour barrel. She said, "I did give Billy the Kid several meals when he would come to our place—I felt so sorry for them when they said they were hungry." The Lesnetts sold the mill to the Cree family in 1887. (Courtesy of the late Carmon Phillips.)

Wealthy young Englishman John Henry Tunstall was drawn to the West by economic opportunity. He and his partner, lawyer Alexander McSween, opened a bank and store in Lincoln, challenging J. J. Dolan and Company's economic domination of the region. His murder in 1878 began the Lincoln County War, as his supporters, "the Regulators," swore revenge on his killers. (Courtesy of the late Carmon Phillips.)

William Bonney, or "Billy the Kid," was brought to the Lincoln County Courthouse in April 1881 after being convicted of killing Sheriff William Brady. Gov. Lew Wallace had agreed to pardon Bonney as part of the general amnesty following the Lincoln County War but did not make good on his promise. Bonney was to be hanged on May 13 but escaped from the two-story adobe building that had been built as headquarters for J. J. Dolan and Company. During the escape, he shot and killed deputies Robert Olinger and Charlie Bell. Bonney was killed by Sheriff Pat Garrett in July 1881. (Courtesy of the late Carmon Phillips.)

The cowboys on the VV Ranch take a break during a horse roundup in 1896. Former sheriff Pat Garrett, famed for killing the outlaw Billy the Kid, worked as ranch manager for a few years. (Courtesy of the late Carmon Phillips.)

James Cree, wealthy owner of a whiskey distillery in Edinburgh, Scotland, was intrigued by stories of vast land tracts available in the American West. In 1885, he invested in land in Lincoln County and in the Angus VV Ranch. Cree and his partner, retired British army officer Brandon Kirby, imported Angus cattle, but neither the foreign ranchers nor the foreign cattle did especially well in New Mexico. Cree left his land to his sons, and his name is still heard in place names around Ruidoso. (Courtesy of Edinburgh Historic Trust.)

In 1895, Buck Prude operated a store near what became known as Ruidoso Junction. In the photograph, he is holding the hand of his son, Andrew. Prude was appointed the first licensed trader for the Mescalero Apaches in 1902. Andrew became a trader as well, and the two men served in that capacity for more than 40 years. (Courtesy of New Mexico State University Library Archives and Special Collections.)

In 1904, the post office was moved from the mill to Highway 70, the road to Alamogordo. Buck Prude served as postmaster, and he may have moved the post office between this building and his store. (Courtesy of the late Carmon Phillips.)

This photograph is one of the earliest of Ruidoso. The winter scene shows Buck Prude's store and post office in the center of the line of buildings. (Courtesy of Historical Center for Southeast New Mexico.)

Abundant rain and snow on Sierra Blanca supported the growth of large conifers. Many sawmills operated in the Ruidoso area. Timber from the forests supported the mining industry and the railroad, which reached Lincoln County in 1879. (Courtesy of the late Carmon Phillips.)

One of the area's early sawmills was the W. R. White sawmill, built in 1918 at the entrance to Upper Canyon. A by-product of squaring the trees to make lumber was the creation of bark-covered "slabs." Early cabins were often covered with slab siding. White once refused to sell some of the siding to a customer because, he said, "If I sell it to you, what would I do when the next customer wanted some?" The building technique continued into the 1950s, as shown by the Seiler family cabin, which was built in 1944. (Above courtesy of Eleanor Bonnell; below courtesy of the Seiler estate.)

In the desert Southwest, it is always the attraction of water that draws people. The mountain climate has always been the Ruidoso area's most important asset. (Courtesy of Mickey Cochran.)

# Two

# A Little Town Grows Bigger

Charles Wingfield and his family arrived in Ruidoso in a covered wagon in 1884. They had come from Texas and were perhaps on their way to White Oaks, where gold had been discovered five years earlier. Wingfield took a job at the mill, managing it for Frank Lesnett and later the Cree family. Four children were born in the mill, including Isaac "Ike" Wingfield, who would become an important public figure in Ruidoso.

New Mexico achieved statehood in 1912, and two years later, Judge Edward Medler and his wife, Lillian, made a trip to what she later called "Ruidoso country." They camped in Upper Canyon near a large rock and wished they could build a cabin on the same spot. Negotiations with Lord Cree, who owned the land, resulted in three cabins being built in 1915. In 1922, Amelia Church of Lincoln opened Singing Pines Cabins, the first commercial cabin operation in Upper Canyon, although business advisors called it "economic insanity." The Ruidoso Lodge followed in 1924. Warren Barrett opened a small grocery store near the entrance to Upper Canyon and built a few small cabins.

More summer cabins were built, all on land leased from the Cree family. Finally, in 1934, seven families bought 40 acres and formed the Ruidoso Cabin Owners. Each family is a shareholder, and stock can only be sold to other family members. The unusual arrangement has preserved the original beauty of the forest and river.

In 1929, artists Peter Hurd and Henriette Wyeth came to Ruidoso for their honeymoon. In a letter, Hurd wrote of "tall woods of pine and spruce and occasional groves of aspen trees trembling in the sunlight, and a trout stream that tumbles down among rocks, glides past heavy ferns along mossy banks and seems to be forever rejoicing there." The couple lived on a ranch in San Patricio and painted many scenes of life in the Hondo Valley and Ruidoso.

The Gateway area was so named perhaps because it was the first point at which visitors could see could see their destination—Sierra Blanca. It was referred to as "Palmer Gateway" after George McCarty and his brother-in-law, Joe Palmer, purchased the large tract of land from the Cree family in the 1940s. The photograph was taken in 1913. (Courtesy of Patricia Huckins.)

Not all campers were interested in roughing it. In 1890, the *Pecos Valley Register* reported that a party of eight people had set off from Roswell on a camping trip along the Rio Ruidoso, noting that the adventurers were supplied with all the necessities, including musical instruments, cards, and fishing tackle. In 1896, James F. Hinkle, who would be elected mayor of Roswell in 1905 and governor of New Mexico in 1923, climbed Sierra Blanca's 12,000-foot peak. From the top are Hinkle, John Hinkle, Dr. Joyner (left), and Dr. Adair (right). (Courtesy of Historical Center for Southeast New Mexico.)

By 1907, a primitive road connected Roswell and Alamogordo. Early road construction was done by teams of horses dragging a "Fresno"—a metal scraper. The trip was still far from comfortable. Jack Hull, who later opened Ye Olde Pyne Tavern and also served as Ruidoso's postmaster and mayor, remembered the trip from Roswell in 1925: "The road was pretty bad—we lost a wheel on the car." (Courtesy of Eleanor Bonnell.)

The Wingfield family home and the Dowlin mill were the only structures in Ruidoso for many years. This house was built in 1929 and was still standing in 2009. The chimney was added in 1931. The Wingfields also built a large dance hall next to their house. A 1932 issue of the *Ruidoso Herald* noted that both the Miss Ruidoso Beauty Pageant and the American Legion were held at "Wingfield Hall." (Courtesy of the Wingfield family.)

Della Wingfield Hale later said, "What started bringing people to this area was babies sick from the summer heat. They would stop at my mother's place to buy milk. A heavy wooden gate was in our front yard. The mothers offered me a nickel to open and close the gate. I lost no time in holding out my hand for the coin. This is what started me in business." Her mother, the enterprising Lula Wingfield, also rented out rooms and offered baths. (Courtesy of the Wingfield family.)

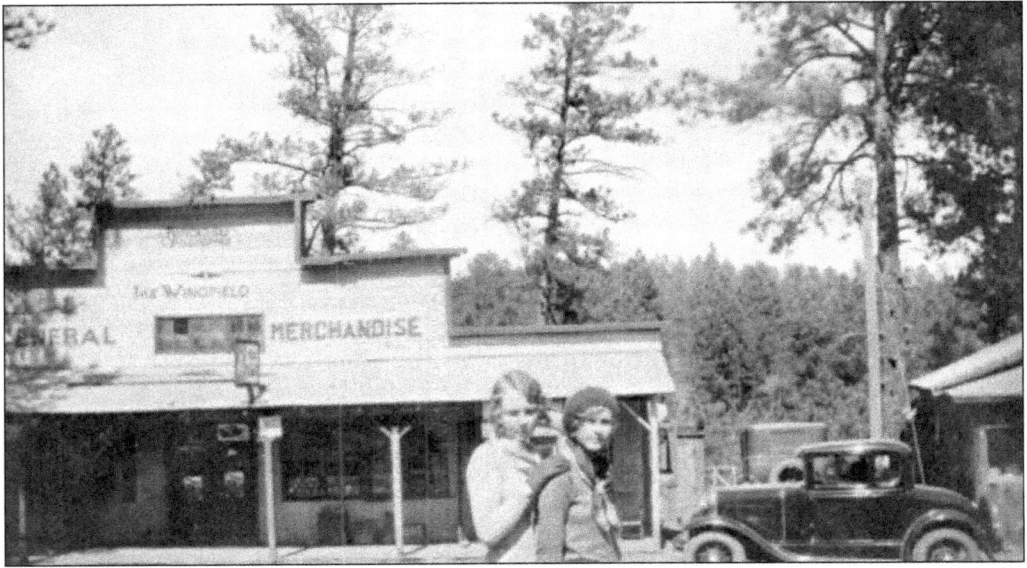

In 1921, Ike Wingfield moved the post office to his store, across the road from his house. At that time, he rode horseback to Fort Stanton once a week to pick up the mail—a trip that took all day. A barbershop was added to the building's east side in 1922 and a meat market in 1923. Opal Wingfield (left) poses with an unidentified friend. (Courtesy of the Wingfield family.)

Ike Wingfield served two terms as Ruidoso's mayor and was the postmaster from 1921 until 1937. He operated a general store and dairy, but he reportedly had a casual attitude about business. A customer in his store wanted to buy a Hershey bar but was told, "I haven't got any more. They just sold so fast that I quit bothering with them." A generous man, Wingfield offered 99-year leases to people who wanted to build summer cabins. The photograph of him and the bear was taken in 1947. Wingfield died in 1954. (Courtesy of the Wingfield family.)

The McDaniel family rented Judge Medler's cabin and requested that, if he wanted to sell it, they would have first chance. Their chance came in 1933 during the Roosevelt Bank Holiday. Medler telegraphed that if McDaniel had $250 cash, he would send the deed. The McDaniels named the cabin Rainbow Oaks for the oak tree that naturally arched over it. (Courtesy of Robyn Fleenor.)

The first three summer cabins in Upper Canyon were built in 1915 by Carrizozo builder Frank English. They were made of wood, with four small sleeping rooms and a stone fireplace, made of river rock. The man who built the fireplace promised, "If it ever smokes, you won't have to pay me a cent." (Courtesy of Robyn Fleenor.)

A "gentleman fisherman" in the style of Izaak Walton, Ernest McDaniel Sr. kept his family supplied with German brown trout caught in the Rio Ruidoso, which flowed just a few yards from his front porch. He once caught a 22-inch trout that he took to an El Paso taxidermist. He kept detailed records of his daily catch, both in notebooks and on the builder's paper that lined his cabin's walls. Anglers enjoyed a limit of 25 fish per day. (Both courtesy of Robyn Fleenor.)

Morning's catch from Ruidoso Stream.

In June 1950, the enormous spruce in the McDaniel yard fell. The tree was 160 feet tall and 5 feet in diameter. It was estimated to be at least 350 years old. The McDaniel family kept a slice of it on their cabin porch. Another large tree measured more than 19 feet in circumference in 1958. (Courtesy of Robyn Fleenor.)

Dr. R. R. Stewart and his brother, Dr. R. A. Stewart, both dentists in El Paso, bought this cabin near the entrance to Upper Canyon in 1922. The photograph was taken in 1926. A dam that diverted irrigation water to the Wingfield Ditch was on the property. The cabin survived the floods of 1941 and 2008 and is essentially unchanged. (Courtesy of Sharon Stewart.)

The Odd Fellows camp in Cedar Creek (above) was built by the El Paso Odd Fellows in 1924. It was used as a summer camp for El Paso's Southwestern Children's Home until 1926, when the Wingfield family donated 10 acres of pasture land near the middle of town and another camp (below) was built. Children enjoyed a mountain vacation until the facility burned in the late 1970s. The Odd Fellows Lodge burned in 1946. (Above courtesy of Herb Brunell; below courtesy of the Wingfield family.)

Navajo Lodge, Ruidoso, N.M.

In 1924, Bob and Edith Boyce opened the first Navajo Lodge with a few small cabins and a dining hall. "There was no water or electricity," Edith remembered. "We carried water in buckets up from the river." The couple leased 10 acres of land for $25 a year. "We had a 25-year lease," Edith said. "That seemed like an awful long time." Edith's father was Lincoln County pioneer Frank Coe, and the Coe Ranch had always been known for its hospitality. (Courtesy of Herb Brunell.)

Horseback riding and miniature golf were attractions for early visitors. The ubiquitous Wingfield girls (Opal, left, and Della, right) enjoy themselves at the Navajo Lodge's miniature golf course. (Courtesy of the Wingfield family.)

Edith Boyce, owner of the Navajo Lodge with her husband, Bob, was usually dressed in riding attire. She was reputed to be an excellent cook. The Navajo Lodge dining room was very popular, with the Boyces serving family-style meals that included their own milk, butter, eggs, and meat. "We charged 50¢ a meal," Edith said. "If we had a good Sunday dinner, we'd start to build another cabin." The Boyces ran cattle on land leased from the Cree family, an open area that became Cree Meadows Country Club. (Courtesy of Herb Brunell.)

Wildlife viewing has always been one of Ruidoso's attractions. Deer, bear, and elk are frequently sighted, although modern visitors are less likely than this man to get quite this close. The photograph was taken at Parsons Hotel, built near the Parsons mine north of Ruidoso. (Courtesy of Herb Brunell.)

Most early visitors simply camped in any open area, and it was common to see clotheslines strung between trees. John Sigler remembered, "A man had some tents set up along the river below Midtown. The tents had a wooden floor and walls built up about three feet—I remember I could just see over the top. The roof and sides were canvas. We would come up from Roswell in the summer and stay there." Water for washing and drinking was hauled from the river or from springs until a public pump was installed on Main Street in the mid-1920s. (Courtesy of Mickey Cochran.)

A troop of Boy Scouts made a camping trip to Ruidoso in 1925. (Courtesy of the Wingfield family.)

The real estate business got an early start in Ruidoso. (Courtesy of Herb Brunell.)

A variety of seasonal businesses served the needs of summer visitors in an area above the Rio Ruidoso that became known as "Midtown." Commercial activity appears a bit slow in the mid-1920s, but the snow on Sierra Blanca suggests that the summer "high season" has not started. (Courtesy of Herb Brunell.)

This stretch of Main Road (now Sudderth Drive) is between Eagle Drive and Center Street. Edith Boyce remembered, "We'd try to open [the Navajo Lodge] by May 15 but we always closed the day after Labor Day because you were worn out and besides everybody was gone. (Courtesy of Mickey Cochrane.)

The Most beautiful Golf Course in America Ruidoso.

The Ruidoso Golf Course, the town's first golf course, opened in the Gateway area in the early 1930s. Longtime resident Wayne Joyce remembered working as a caddy: "It was mostly just whatever grass was growing, but they did mow the fairways. The 'greens' were sand, and they'd put some oil on them to keep the dust down. When someone was ready to putt, we'd smooth a path from the ball to the hole and make a little ridge on each side, so it was almost like playing miniature golf." He added, "I got 25 cents a round." (Courtesy of Herb Brunell.)

Any occasion is a good excuse for a parade in Ruidoso. Opal Wingfield occupies the throne on this wagon moving down Main Road in 1932. Her sister, Della, sits at the right. (Courtesy of the Wingfield family.)

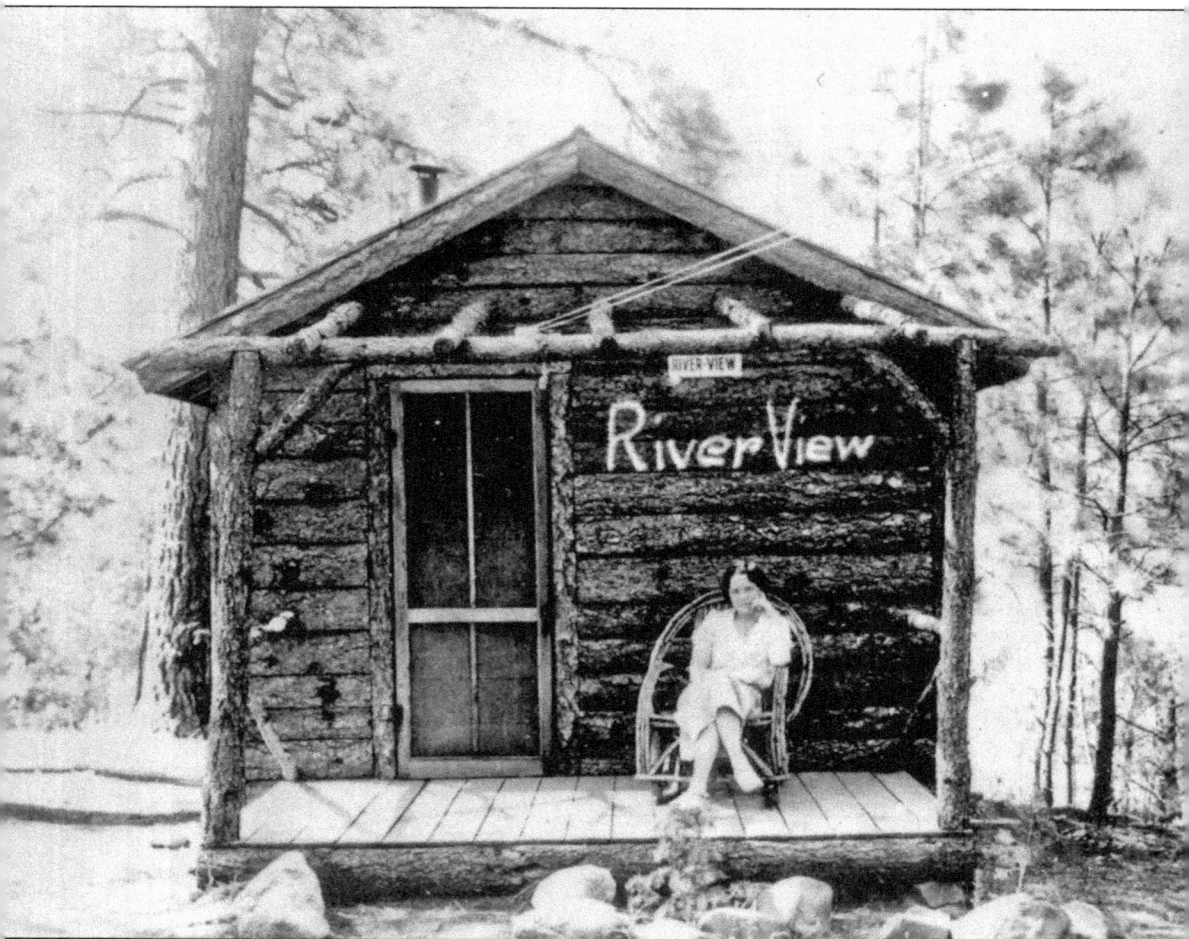

Early cabins were built close to the river—so close that one could fish from the porch. Farming families brought wagonloads of produce, milk, and butter to the canyon entrance. The children would run up and down the river, taking orders and delivering groceries to the cabin occupants, earning as much as $10 a day. (Courtesy of Herb Brunell.)

# Three

# HAPPY TIMES IN THE
# GREAT DEPRESSION

Although roughly one-third of New Mexico's population was unemployed during the Depression, the town grew significantly during the decade. Young men in the Civilian Conservation Corps built a camp at Cedar Creek and a stone lookout tower on Monjeau Peak.

In the early 1930s, Warren H. Barrett, who owned cabins and a small grocery store, published a small pamphlet called the *Ruidoso News*. One issue proclaimed, "After breathing the cool, bracing mountain air, sleeping under woolen blankets and drinking cold spring water, one cannot help but wonder whether it is still hot and uncomfortable back home." Another news item noted that about 20 percent of the town's cabins had electricity.

The electricity was provided by a small power plant, built in 1926. It only ran a few hours a day, and by sundown, it was "lights out." The plant operator supposedly cut the power momentarily as a signal it was about to be shut off, but according to Wayne Joyce, "You could hear the diesel engine all over town—if you couldn't hear the engine, you knew you didn't have power."

Referring to another kind of electricity, the *Ruidoso News* cautioned against attaching radio antennae to trees, noting that lightning had struck one such arrangement, throwing a woman from her bed, breaking windows, splintering wooden walls, and destroying the radio.

Some local women began the first women's chamber of commerce in the United States. "The main thing we did was collect the garbage," Edith Boyce remembered. "We bought an old truck and hired a young man. We charged $3 a month to collect garbage. I'd get on my horse and ride around, collecting the money." A big town improvement came in 1938, when Main Road was paved from the Junction to the intersection of Alto Road (later Mechem Drive).

A new attraction in town was the "talking pictures." A tent theater in the Skyland area showed films like Zane Grey's *Laska of the Rio Grande*. Admission was 35¢.

Dr. Dan D. Swearingin, a Roswell physician, built cabins in 1938 to provide a summer job for his 15-year-old son, Dan Jr. Like most lodging facilities, the cabins were primitive, with kerosene lamps and water hauled from a spring. Guests brought their own mattresses and linens. Fathers came up on weekends, but the rest of the family would often spend the entire summer by the river. Dan D. Swearingin Jr. later said, "Ruidoso came into its own during the Depression."

In 1930, Bert and Sydney Bonnell opened a dude ranch at their 1882 family home in the Hondo Valley east of Ruidoso. Advertisements in the *Chicago Tribune* promised room, board, and a horse to ride for $40 a month. Prospective clients wrote to ask what sort of weapons they needed to bring in case of Native American attacks. Sydney's father was Frank Coe, and her sister was Edith Boyce, owner of Ruidoso's Navajo Lodge. Many guests came year after year. The 1934 guest book shows visitors from Chicago, Los Angeles, and Washington, D.C. In 1946, the *Ruidoso News* remarked, "The Bonnell Ranch continues to welcome, with a warm handshake, the cowpuncher in his boots or the man from a distant city." (Courtesy of Eleanor Bonnell.)

Cousins Frank (left) and George Coe pose at the Bonnell Ranch about 1929. The Coes were friends of Billy the Kid, and although they tried to remain neutral during the Lincoln County War, George lost his trigger finger during the gun battle at Blazer's Mill. He washed the wound in the Rio Ruidoso and later claimed that its successful healing proved the river's health benefits. (Courtesy of Eleanor Bonnell.)

Eleanor Bonnell, granddaughter of Bert and Sydney Bonnell, remembered, "Every Saturday night, they'd take the furniture out of the dining room and have a dance. All the people who lived on nearby ranches would be there, as well as the guests." In the photograph below, Bob Boyce is dancing at left. In the photograph above, Sydney Bonnell is at the piano, writer Dan Storm is playing the guitar, and Clifford Casey is playing fiddle. Although not pictured here, artist and neighbor Peter Hurd often played the guitar. (Both courtesy of Eleanor Bonnell.)

In the mid-1920s, the little grocery store and gas station at Ruidoso Junction offered the only gasoline between Roswell and Alamogordo. Ike Wingfield bought the store in 1927 and hired Clayton Bennett to run it. (Courtesy of Betty Bennett.)

In 1926, Clayton Bennett's family put him on a train heading west, according to his daughter, Betty Bennett. "He had never been more than 12 miles from Warren, Indiana," she said, "but he had tuberculosis and they didn't know what else to do for him. He had enough money to get to Tularosa, New Mexico. They shipped his casket along with him." When he got off the train, a doctor took him to a modest sanatorium, where he rested for three months. He began to recover and worked odd jobs, one of which took him to Ruidoso, where he stayed the rest of his life. He returned to Indiana in 1933 to marry Helen McClurg. They pose with their daughter, Betty, in 1941. (Courtesy of Betty Bennett.)

"We were the only motel at that end of town," Betty Bennett said of her family's business, located on Highway 70. "People staying at the cabins would buy apples in the Hondo Valley and leave them in their cars. The bears would come and steal the apples. Mother would run out with her dishrag to chase them off." (Courtesy of Betty Bennett.)

Betty Bennett grew up pumping gas, changing tires, and painting rocks to sell in the gift shop. She remembers, "Every kid in town painted rocks at one time or another for Daddy." The photograph shows the interior of the shop in the early 1950s. From left to right are Helen, Betty, Clayton, and an unidentified man. (Courtesy of Betty Bennett.)

This photograph of Midtown, taken in the mid-1930s, shows a few more businesses. The tall pine tree in the middle of the photograph is said to have been the "jail tree." In 1947, the *Ruidoso News*, noting the construction of Ruidoso's first jail, said, "Current routine followed by village peace officers is to chain any drunk who 'gets too drunk' to a tree or post, whichever is handy, until he sobers up." (Courtesy of Mickey Cochran.)

In 1932, a visitor wrote, "To a seasoned tourist who has motored over much of North America's scenic highways and visited many of its beauty spots and playgrounds, the charm of the Ruidoso and its environs grows with each day's sojourn." (Courtesy of Herb Brunell.)

COTTAGE EAT SHOP RUIDOSO N.M.

Della Wingfield opened the Cottage Eat Shop in the mid-1920s. The restaurant stood at the northeast corner of what are now Sudderth and Mechem Drives. (Both courtesy of the Wingfield family.)

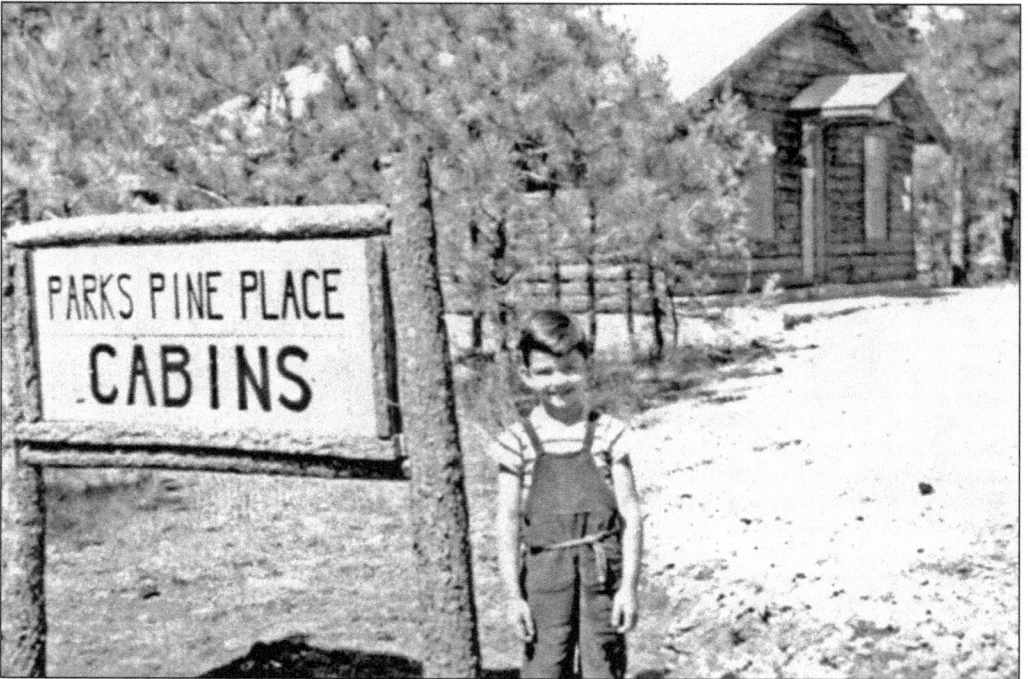

Nell Crain Parks (below) taught school in Texas in 1931, being paid mostly in scrip—printed money that could only be used locally. Thinking she could do better, she came to New Mexico, staying in a cabin at H. E. Carter's 40 acres. The enterprising Carter sold her some land in Upper Canyon, and she lived in a tent while her cabin was being built. Her son Dave Parks (above) remembered, "The house was built on a steep slope, so one side was up on stilts. Mother asked the carpenter how much it would cost to enclose it and make another room. He said it would cost $50, adding, 'Those boys of mine eat so much, they can do that.' Then she asked how much it would cost to add a fireplace, and he said $35 and that 'those boys can haul the rocks up from the river.' " (Both courtesy of Dave Parks.)

In 1923, entrepreneur Horace E. Carter bought 80 acres of land in what would become the Midtown area of Ruidoso. Two years later, he sold 40 acres to Roswell's New Mexico Military Institute, who built the Carrizo Lodge as a summer retreat for their cadets. Carter operated a cabin rental and grocery store and sold off the land in small parcels for summer cabins. This building stood at the 2009 location of Compass Bank. (Courtesy of Mickey Cochran.)

Harry and Bessie Gottlieb operated Harry's Picture Place from their home on Ruidoso's Main Road. The photograph was taken in 1927. (Courtesy of the late Carmon Phillips.)

After passing Apache Summit, Highway 70 (the road from El Paso) descended into Dark Canyon, a place of thick forests and treacherous mud holes. Lloyd Davis remembered that on family trips, they would start early on winter mornings: "We wouldn't even attempt it if the road wasn't frozen." Highway 70 was paved in the early 1940s as part of the war effort. (Courtesy of Mickey Cochran.)

# *Four*

# THERE'S A WAR ON!

World War II provided a new clientele for the Ruidoso area—servicemen from nearby military installations. "The G.I.s weren't allowed to wear civvies," Dave Parks remembered, "so the main street in town would just be a sea of khaki on the weekends." In 1941, the highway between El Paso and Ruidoso was completely paved.

Van R. Parker was stationed in nearby Alamogordo, learning to fly B-29s. In his memoir of World War II, he wrote, "Girl chasing was a popular pastime and a popular place was Ruidoso. Ruidoso was a beautiful village in picturesque mountainous country some 40 miles northeast of Alamogordo. If you wanted to breathe fresh air in a place of scenic beauty and enjoy female companionship, Ruidoso was it."

The barracks at the old Civilian Conservation Corps camp on Cedar Creek was used by shell-shocked pilots as a place to rest and recover. German prisoners of war from Fort Stanton were brought down to cook and clean for them.

Gambling was as popular with the soldiers as it was with civilians. It was technically illegal, but business owners with slot machines, poker tables, and roulette wheels devised ways to disguise them. Dave Parks remembered, "There were slot machines everywhere—bars, restaurants, grocery stores. Some of them were in beaverboard cabinets with a door in front. Others were on wheels. The owners usually knew when there was going to be a raid, so they would just close them up or turn them around."

In 1946, the village marshal resigned, saying the job was the "most troublesome" of any he had ever had. A visitor leaving a Ruidoso nightspot reportedly said, "That is a place where they have what it takes to take what you have." As Bill McCarty put it, "It was the fun you could have in town that made Ruidoso."

In 1949, the New Mexico Press Association met in Ruidoso. The reporters undoubtedly enjoyed themselves but went home to write stories about the "utter lawlessness and lack of law enforcement prevailing in that colorful mountain resort." A shocked *Albuquerque Journal* reporter wrote that "all sorts of gambling was wide open and bars operated on Sunday," and the reporter from Carlsbad noted, "In most places of business the slot machines were operating full blast, and a car parked in front was marked 'chief of police.' "

Word spread quickly when the authorities planned a raid. Las Cruces judge James McGhee, in town to oversee a raid, reported that a little girl approached him as he ate lunch and asked "Are you the man who has come here to take away the slot machines?" The state police occasionally managed to pull off a raid, hauling away the slot machines and busting up the poker tables and roulette wheels in the middle of Main Road.

wn Ruidoso, New Mexico

In 1946, *Ruidoso News* publisher Lloyd Bloodworth wrote in an editorial, "The tourist business is our greatest industry and brings more cold cash than any other. We are saps if we don't take advantage of it." The Covered Wagon Curio Shop, one of the town's oldest businesses, is in the lower right of the photograph. (Courtesy of Herb Brunell.)

Construction of the "new" Navajo Lodge began in 1938. The three-story, Pueblo Revival–style inn had beamed ceilings and a kiva fireplace that heated most of the building. For decades, nearly every important social event took place at the Navajo Lodge. Louise Coe, the first woman elected to the state legislature in 1927 and the only woman to serve during her four years in office, was a frequent guest. The *Roswell Record* noted, "Saturday night at the Navajo Lodge in Ruidoso a weekly dance is held in which couples come from a radius of 100 miles away. Many of the dancers are not aware that the pretty young woman presiding at the piano is a state senator." During World War II, correspondent Ernie Pyle spent a week at the lodge. (Courtesy of Mickey Cochran.)

The lobby of the Navajo Lodge was typical of the inn's casual elegance. The River Room was built with a view of the Rio Ruidoso; the Buffalo Room had a mural painted by artist Reynolds Jones. (Courtesy of Mickey Cochran.)

The Navajo Lodge was the center of social and political life in Ruidoso for several decades. An advertisement in the 1955 telephone book announced that the Navajo Lodge is "The Center of Everything in Ruidoso." Since it was the only building in town that could accommodate a large group of people, the claim was essentially true. "Just before the war, I had at least one convention every month of the year come to the lodge," Edith Boyce said. (Courtesy of Herb Brunell.)

After the Boyces' son Bobby returned from World War II, a cocktail lounge was added off the lobby. (Courtesy of the late Carmon Phillips.)

The same stretch of Main Road shows quite a difference between spring (indicated by the snow on Sierra Blanca) and summer. (Above courtesy of Mickey Cochran; below courtesy of Herb Brunell.)

Carmon and Leona Phillips moved to Ruidoso, where her family had a cabin, after World War II. They leased and later bought Dowlin's Mill and built a small house next to it that also served as a photograph shop. "Most of my time in Ruidoso has been spent trying to make a living," Carmon said. (Courtesy of the late Carmon Phillips.)

This structure was built to cover the town's original water pump. The photograph was taken before 1938. Bill Hart organized the town's first municipal water system in 1940, using the original well. There were several riding stables right in town, with horses and automobiles sharing the streets. (Courtesy of Herb Brunell.)

A popular feature of the *Ruidoso News* was "Canyon Echoes," a chronicle of visitors: "Mrs. F. C. Conner and Lucile Ford of Forth Worth are visiting for the months of July and August. They are staying in the Dan Dee Cabins." "Mr. and Mrs. P. H. Simmonds of Lubbock, Texas, have their little grandson with them on their vacation in Ruidoso. They are in the Autry Cabins." (Courtesy of the late Carmon Phillips.)

The Noisy Water Lodge was built and enlarged from 1936 to 1940. Located near the end of Upper Canyon, its nightlife attracted less attention than the Midtown establishments. "It was where you went on important dates," Betty Bennett remembered. (Courtesy of Mickey Cochran.)

EL TAOS COURT—RUIDOSO N.MEX. 13 MODERN UNITS IN THE TALL PINES
7000 FEET ELEVATION                    MR. AND MRS. GEORGE BONAL OWNER—MGRS.

More modern accommodations appeared in town, many of them built in the popular Pueblo Revival style. The former El Taos Court Motel was still in use in 2009, although the motel rooms had been converted to small shops. (Courtesy of Mickey Cochran.)

P-213 RUIDOSO CLUB HOUSE AND CAFE-RUIDOSO.N.M.

The Ruidoso Clubhouse and Café was built by Jack Hull in the late 1930s. It was one of the many establishments that offered gambling as a sideline. Joetyne Wright remembered going to the café on her lunch break and playing the slot machines. (Courtesy of Mickey Cochran.)

Frank Barajas stands by the jukebox in the Mint Bar in September 1946. Barajas served first as night watchman and became village marshal in 1947. *New Mexico Law* magazine described him as "calm, even-tempered, quietly going about his job of keeping law and order in the Playground of the Southwest." (Courtesy Helen Barajas Woodfin.)

Joetyne Wright called the Ruidoso Bar "a good place to go to have a fight. It was the toughest bar in town." One of its advertised attractions in the early 1950s was cockfighting. (Courtesy of Herb Brunell.)

In 1946, the *Ruidoso News* noted, "The old timers can scarcely believe what they see and what is happening to their once isolated paradise. We are in the middle of an unprecedented boom that can make or break the future destiny of Ruidoso." (Photograph by Robert Hand, courtesy of Stephanie Morgan.)

The community celebrated Pioneer Caravans in June 1940. An enormous pit barbecue smoldered in Schoolhouse Park, tended by the young men from the Civilian Conservation Corps camp in Cedar Creek. The chamber of commerce called the event "a throwback to the glamorous frontier days in the scenic one-time home of Billy the Kid." (Courtesy of Wayne Joyce.)

An estimated 6,000 to 10,000 people enjoyed Western music, square dancing, parades, Mescalero Apache dancers, and a rodeo. (Courtesy of Wayne Joyce.)

The oxen and the wooden cart, or *carreta* in Spanish, came from the Bonnell Ranch. Ralph Bonnell built the carreta and left it out in the rain to weather. The Pioneer Caravans program proclaimed, "Howdy folks! We're powerful glad y'all dropped in to help us celebrate that summer 400 years ago, when Coronado and his hard-ridin' waddies first sprinkled shod hoofs on this here range. It's been a heap of work for a little outfit like us to put on such a roundup and free dinner, but we'll allow our wages have been paid if y'all just show us some of those big Western grins that mean you're having' a good time." (Both courtesy of the late Carmon Phillips.)

Montie's Riding Academy, near the entrance to Upper Canyon, was one of several in Ruidoso. Riding was a popular activity. All-day trips to Sierra Blanca went up through Upper Canyon, across the Mescalero Reservation and up to the high alpine meadows, or "parks." The most intrepid could climb the peak on foot. As a teenager, Martha Ann Gardenhire guided trips to "Baldy" several times a week. "We crossed the river 14 times before we got up the mountain," she remembered. If I had kids in the group, we'd stop and pick wild raspberries." (Above courtesy of Herb Brunell; below courtesy of Marty DiSanto.)

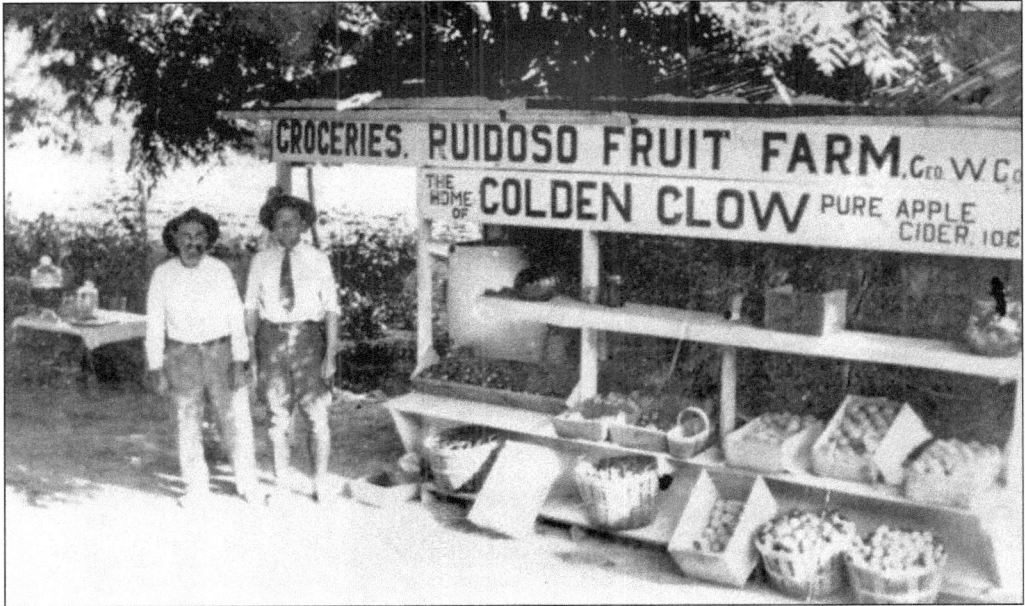

The Coe family settled in the Hondo Valley below Ruidoso in the early 1870s. In 1925, they opened their first roadside fruit stand, selling apples, plums, and apricots. George Coe (above left) and his son, William, sell fruit and copies of George's book, *Frontier Fighter*. Wilbur Coe remembered, "It stood under a huge cottonwood that sheltered it from the sun, and on a hot summer day, it was an inviting place to stop and cool the engine of the auto and get some fruit to take along on the trip. Cars were few and far between, and waits for customers were long. There was plenty of time to talk to the tourists. . . . The day is gone when the motorist hot, tired and dusty from the road, would turn an apple box on end and pass the time of day for an hour or so." Ralph Bonnell (below left) and Bert Pfingsten work at the Hondo Valley Apple Cooperative. (Both courtesy of Eleanor Bonnell.)

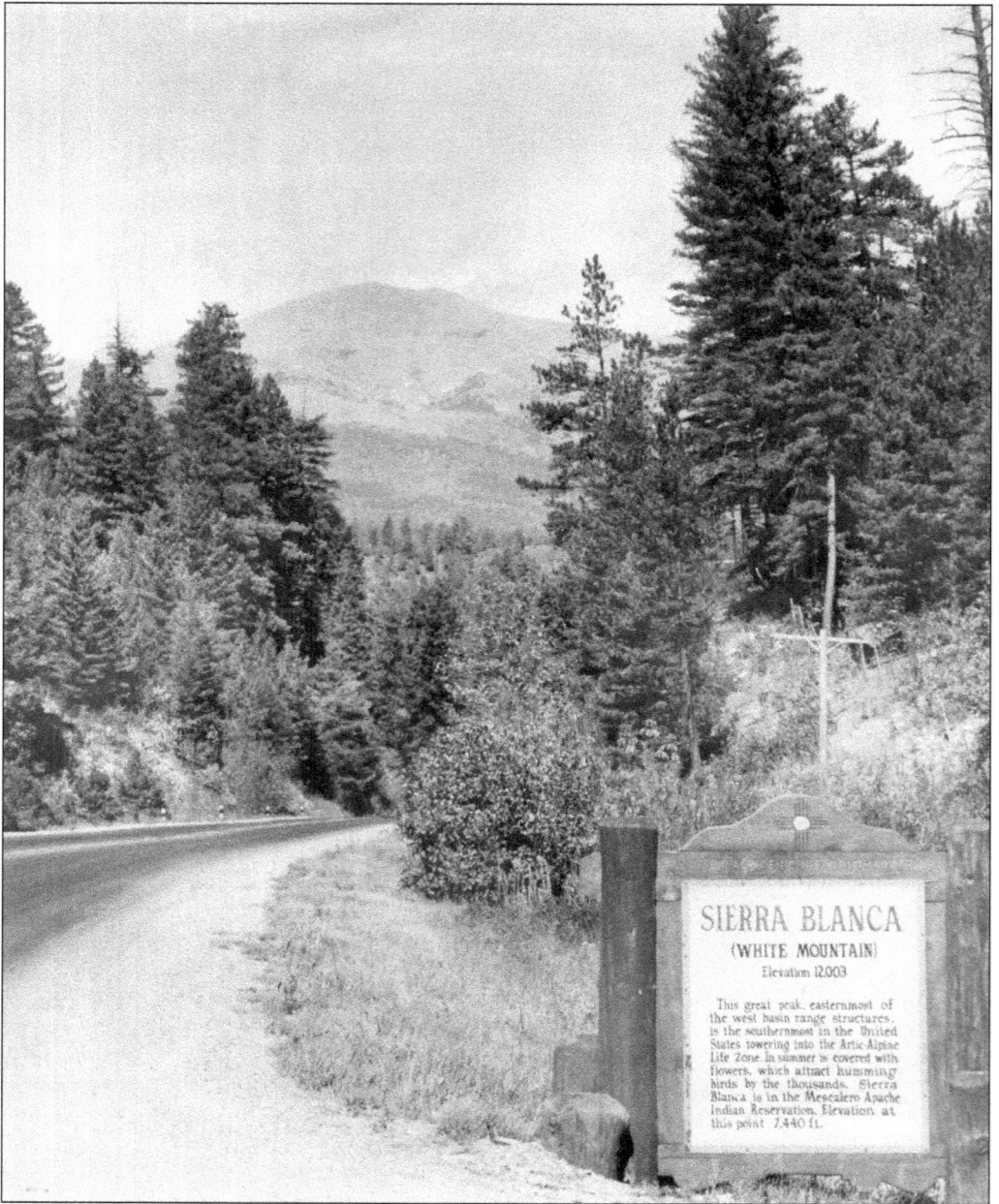

Travelers on Highway 70 enjoy a stunning view of Sierra Blanca as the road descends from Apache Summit. The mountain then seems to disappear, only to reappear as one enters the Gateway area of Ruidoso. (Courtesy of the late Carmon Phillips.)

## Five

# PLAYGROUND OF THE SOUTHWEST

The end of gas rationing and a general optimism and feeling of adventure put Americans on the highways in unprecedented numbers. By 1954, the highway from El Paso to Alamogordo was completely paved.

A commercial for Chevrolet urged everyone to "see the USA in your Chevrolet." Families visited national parks in record numbers. Visits to the Lincoln National Forest increased from 178,000 in 1950 to 914,000 in 1959.

Ruidoso business owners and community leaders threw themselves into the challenge of telling the world about the wonders of Ruidoso. Speeches and newspaper articles repeated the belief that "Ruidoso has what it takes to build the biggest and best resort city in the Rockies or the entire Southwest," as a *Ruidoso News* editorial noted in 1946.

In the 1930s, the town adopted the slogan "Playground of the Southwest," although the newspaper wryly remarked in 1954 that the "playground" could use a face lift to take care of the "ankle-deep mud through which pedestrians must wade."

Movie stars began to show up, like Dale Robertson, Chill Wills, and Robert Mitchum, who supposedly got in a fight at the Win, Place, and Show bar. In 1954, Linda Darnell bought a ranch outside Picacho, near her friends the Hurds. The celebrity was "seen frequently in our grocery stores, our night spots and our beauty parlors." Radio personality Paul Harvey visited Ruidoso in 1974 and announced in his broadcast, "The downtown of Ruidoso is one street wide and seven miles long."

An official racetrack near the community of Hollywood offered a legal form of gambling. New golf courses and drive-in theaters opened, and winter sports brought another kind of visitor with the opening of Sierra Blanca Ski Area in 1961.

On the Fourth of July 1960, Ruidoso had record crowds. "Traffic in downtown Ruidoso came to a complete stop on several occasions with cars bumper to bumper," the newspaper said.

And in 1960, the local Elks prepared to attend their national convention in Dallas. As their souvenir offering to promote Ruidoso, they went to the racetrack, where they collected and packaged horse droppings from the "fastest horses in the world."

In 1952, Alto Road was paved and renamed Mechem Drive after Gov. Edwin L. Mechem. Dan D. Swearingin holds the shovel in the center of the photograph. The building is a newer version of the Cottage Eat Shop, housing a gift shop. (Courtesy of the late Carmon Phillips.)

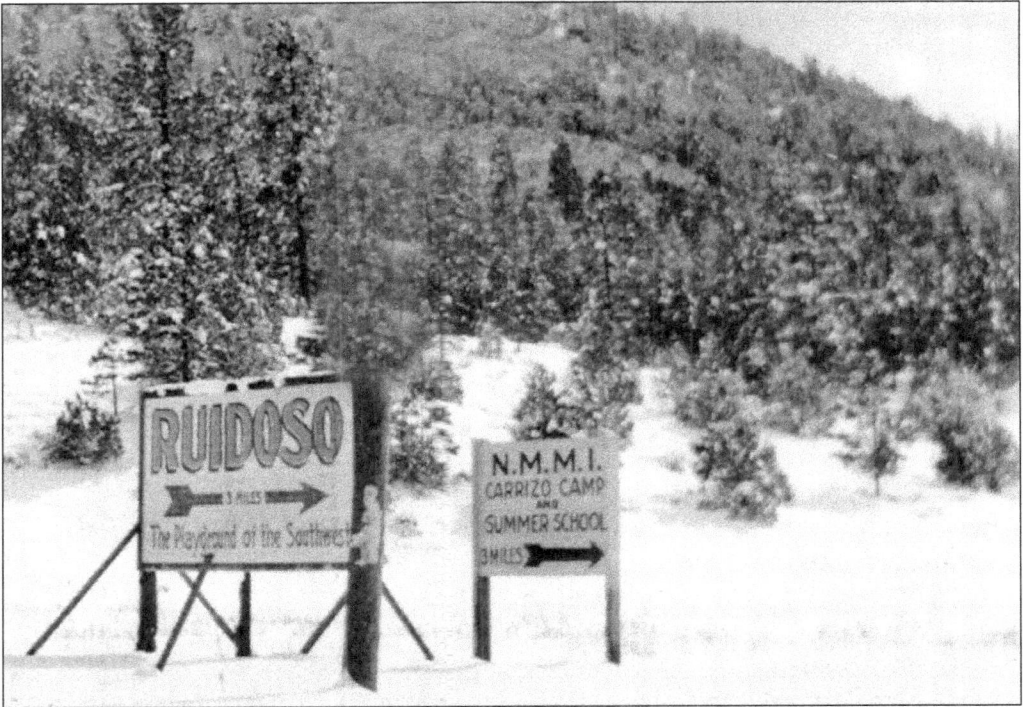

Ruidoso used every opportunity to display its slogan, "Playground of the Southwest." (Courtesy of Mickey Cochran.)

Ruidoso grew along the river, which followed a narrow canyon. The town was several miles from the highway, connected by a road from "the Junction," the town's bus station. A larger access road was built in the 1960s, but the original road remained Junction Road. In 2009, Sierra Blanca Motors stood at the same location. (Courtesy of Herb Brunell.)

Roswell's New Mexico Military Institute built Carrizo Lodge in 1927 to provide "a happy mountain life for the boys." The lodge was built on land H. E. Carter bought from Col. George Purington's widow, Mary, in 1923 for $25 an acre. (Courtesy of the late Carmon Phillips.)

In 1952, Herbert Greggerson, a retired El Paso mailman with sense of whimsy, and his wife, Pauline, bought Carrizo Lodge. The couple were avid square dancers and gave classes and held gatherings at the lodge. They were famous for their "hot rock dinners," cooked on flat rocks heated in an open-pit fire. (Courtesy of Mickey Cochran.)

The swimming pool at Carrizo Lodge was a main attraction to NMMI cadets and other visitors. The lodge and its pool were used by local high school students for a semester until Ruidoso High School opened in 1946. The football team was obliged to take a plunge every afternoon after practice. The pool was spring-fed and extremely cold. (Courtesy of Herb Brunell.)

Artist Frederic Taubes began summer art classes at the Carrizo Lodge in 1955. The artistic atmosphere was enhanced by the Greggersons' large collection of antiques and music boxes. Taubes taught art classes at the lodge until 1976. (Courtesy of the late Carmon Phillips.)

67

The photograph, taken before 1952, shows the intersection of Main Road (Sudderth Drive) and Alto Road (Mechem Drive). The Wingfield home is in the lower left, and the office for the town's electric plant was in the building across the street. (Courtesy of the late Carmon Phillips.)

Carmon Phillips worked tirelessly to promote Ruidoso. His photographs appeared in an article about the town in *Life* magazine in 1954. He resumed production of the magazine *Pictorial Ruidoso* and printed postcards that he sold to other shops. He and his wife, Leona, purchased the abandoned Dowlin mill. Carmon restored the great wheel and opened a curio shop in the adobe building. Advertisements for the shop offer cameras, film, books, records, and watch repair. (Courtesy of the late Carmon Phillips.)

Carmon and Leona Phillips lived with their daughter, Delana, in the small building next to the mill. In 1960, residents voted to make Main Road a four-lane rather than a two-lane road. The decision might have been influenced by the state's reluctance to fund a two-lane road. The name of the road was changed to Sudderth Drive, after the state highway commissioner, John Sudderth. (Courtesy of the late Carmon Phillips.)

The Nob Hill Restaurant advertised "Chew With a View" for its dining room with a view of Sierra Blanca. The Nob Hill Elementary School stood at the same location in 2009. (Courtesy of the late Carmon Phillips.)

Leck Cowden took over the Ruidoso Clubhouse in the 1950s and renamed it Leck's Lanes. He was one of the people who helped run the ski area at Cedar Creek. (Courtesy of Herb Brunell.)

The Davis Bowling Alley was built in 1938 by Lloyd Davis, who later owned the Navajo Lodge. Herb Brunell remembered a job setting pins: "I hated to see the GIs come in, they's throw the balls so hard." (Courtesy of Lloyd Davis Jr.)

The photograph was taken in the early 1950s. The stone building in the background was built in 1941 and has housed a VFW post, a beauty salon, and many gift shops. (Courtesy of the late Carmon Phillips.)

The Central Bar and Grill was one of the town's entertainment and gambling centers. The building in the photograph burned in 1953, and the Central was relocated in the next block. (Courtesy of the late Carmon Phillips.)

In 1948, high school student Helen Barajas was competing for the title of Frontier Days Queen. Voting was by money placed in jars around town. Tommy Hicks, owner of the Central Bar and Grill, promised to put $50 in her jar but was distracted by a raid on the town's gambling establishments. Her rival and best friend, Mary Wimberly, won. (Courtesy of the late Carmon Phillips.)

The new Central Bar and Grill maintained the same ambience as the old one. (Courtesy of the late Carmon Phillips.)

The Capitan High School band performed at the dedication of the Smokey Bear Museum in November 1958. It was perhaps a bit premature—only the front log wall had actually been built. (Courtesy of Mary Guck Crenshaw.)

The completed Smokey Bear Museum opened on July 4, 1960. The museum has expanded over the years, and the original log cabin with its stone fireplace was being used as a gift shop in 2008. (Courtesy of Mary Guck Crenshaw.)

The pageant *The Last Escape of Billy the Kid* was first staged in Lincoln in 1940, with artist Peter Hurd playing Billy. John Davis (right) played "the Kid" for several years in the early 1950s. Louise and Wilbur Coe were instrumental in organizing the pageant and encountered some initial resistance from descendants of participants in the Lincoln County War. The annual outdoor event, with galloping horses, gunfire, and dancing girls, was still being performed in 2009. (Both courtesy of the late Carmon Phillips.)

The chamber of commerce building was replaced in 1997 at the intersection of Sudderth Drive and Carrizo Canyon Road. (Courtesy of Herb Brunell.)

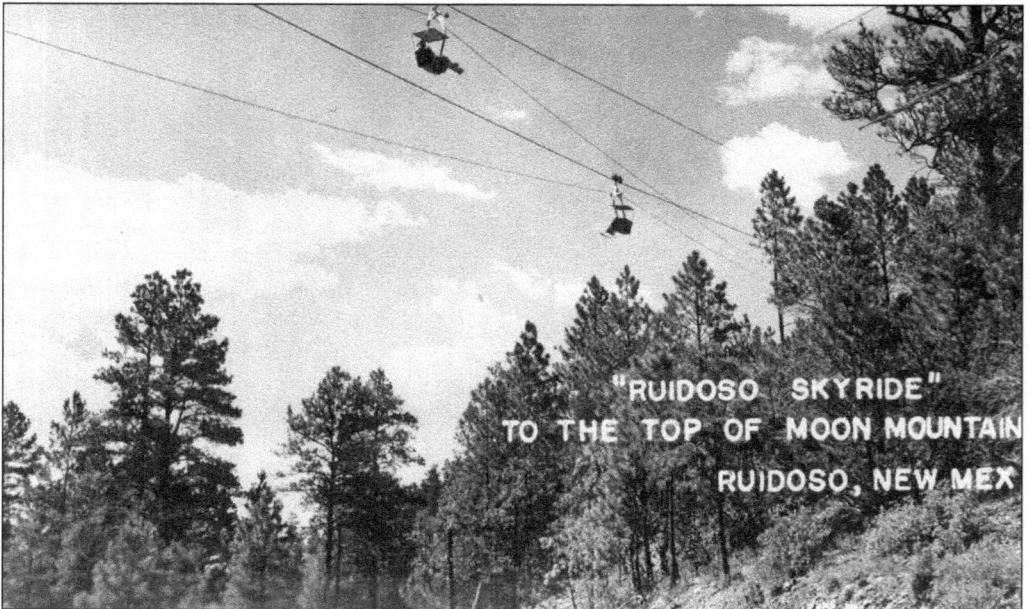

In 1952, the Ruidoso Sky Ride took the adventurous to the top of Moon Mountain. The apparatus had been an aerial ore-transporting tramway in a mine in Magdalene, New Mexico. Tickets were $1 for adults and 50¢ for children. In 1959, a similar ride in Ruidoso Downs took people a mile and a half from Highway 70 to the top of Wildcat Mountain. Attractions included being able to see a race being run at the racetrack. (Courtesy of Herb Brunell.)

George McCarty moved to Ruidoso in 1930 after his brother-in-law, Joe Palmer, passed through the town on vacation. After World War II, the two men bought most of what had been the Cree family's 5,000 acres. They formed White Mountain Development Company and developed golf courses and residential property. The Cree Meadows Golf Course opened in 1946. The clubhouse burned down in 1978 and was rebuilt. (Both courtesy of the late Carmon Phillips.)

The Navajo Lodge was in ruins when this unidentified painter chose it as a subject. The lodge, which had been the social center of Ruidoso for decades, was torn down in 1975. (Courtesy of Herb Brunell.)

A star was hung every Christmas on a tree near the Lookout Tower, where it shone above the town. (Courtesy of Mickey Cochran.)

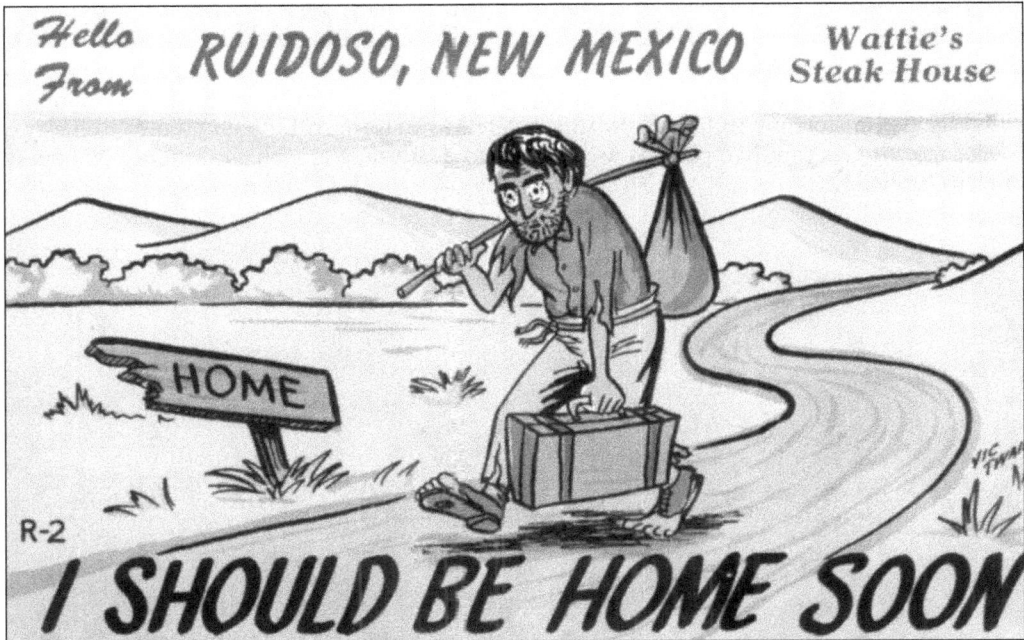

The postcard was printed (and presumably sold) by Wattie's Café, whose newspaper advertisements commented on local events and carried the slogan "Wat's cookin' at Wattie's?" (Courtesy of Mickey Cochran.)

Sierra Blanca's 12,000-foot elevation can create large amounts of both rain and snow. In December 1890, an article in the *Silver City Enterprise* reported that attorney "Col. A. J. Fountain, who had the misfortune to be caught in a severe snow storm in Lincoln County some two weeks ago, reports that five persons were frozen to death during a blizzard there." (Courtesy of Herb Brunell.)

## *Six*

# FUN IN THE SNOW

Most early visitors left town before winter arrived. But locals and some hardier visitors strapped on skis and glided down through Upper Canyon, sometimes all the way to town. During the 1950s, Texas Western University (later the University of Texas at El Paso) held an annual Snow Fiesta, bringing students to Ruidoso to ski and toboggan.

The town's first ski area was opened at the end of Cedar Creek Road in 1938. Skiers could either hike up the short slope or buy a lift ticket and use the gasoline-powered rope tow. Local ski enthusiasts maintained the area and began a campaign to receive permission from the U.S. Forest Service to construct a ski area on Sierra Blanca.

Permission was granted in 1960, and oilman and rancher R. O. Anderson financed the venture. A *Ruidoso News* editorial boasted, "The proposed winter sports area near Ruidoso will be one of the biggest and most ornate outdoor playgrounds in the Southwest, rivaling such existing spas as Sun Valley, Idaho, and Squaw Valley."

Work began with a specially designed four-man cabin, packed in by horseback, assembled, and used to house the first workers. Kingsbury Pitcher of Aspen, Colorado, supervised the construction.

Meanwhile, back in town, a string of celebrities came to promote the ski area, including actress Elinor Donahue (best known for the television series *Father Knows Best*) and actor Dale Robertson. Everyone received a ceremonial pair of skis, which they accepted with varying levels of enthusiasm.

The Sierra Blanca Ski Resort opened in 1961. Its opening was delayed by heavy snowfall, and officials predicted "1,000 skiers each weekend." In December 1961, the new area set a state record for the number of visitors. R. O. Anderson sold the area to the Mescalero Apache tribe in 1963 for $1.75 million.

Nationally, the interest in skiing increased during the 1970s. In 1975, daily lift tickets at Sierra Blanca Ski Resort sold for $9, and a season pass cost $155. A bumper sticker in 1976 proclaimed, "Yes! God wanted Texans to ski. He gave them Ruidoso." In 1985, the Sierra Blanca Ski Resort was renamed "Ski Apache."

Hundreds of thousands of people, the majority of them from Texas, have learned to ski on Sierra Blanca. Family groups return each year, with children and finally grandchildren gliding down the same snow-covered slopes.

In 1941, the *El Paso Times* noted that Ruidoso has "a toboggan slide a half mile long" and that "Ruidoso businessmen have put up $1,000 to install a rope tow." The Ruidoso Club House, operated by Bernard and Marie Rooney, rented toboggans. Lloyd Davis remembered night-time sledding, with tin cans filled with kerosene lining the hill and providing light. (Courtesy of Herb Brunell.)

Ruidoso can experience some surprising weather. For example, 3 feet of snow fell on Labor Day 1936 and 2 feet in April 1949. In December 1987, holiday snow and 50-mile-per-hour winds created 12-foot drifts. (Courtesy of Mickey Cochran.)

The *Ruidoso News* reported that New Year's Day 1950 was "the biggest day for winter sports" in the town's history, with more than 100 skiers and "twice as many onlookers." The rope tow operated for eight consecutive days. "This should wake up the local people to continue to push and push again to get the proposed ski run in White Mountain Park." (Courtesy of the late Carmon Phillips.)

Andy Seiler, an El Paso builder, and his wife, Betty, enjoyed Ruidoso's outdoor life, including skiing at Cedar Creek. (Courtesy of the Seiler estate.)

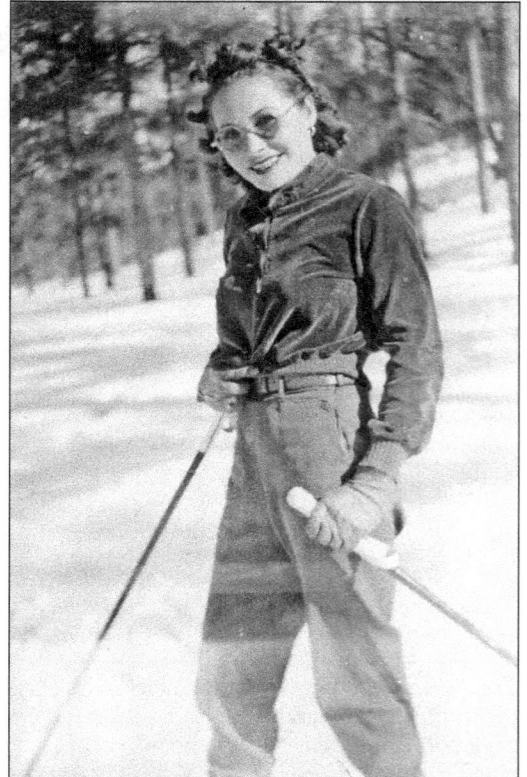

In addition to skiing, Betty Seiler enjoyed hunting and fishing. The couple built a cabin and spent much of their time in Ruidoso. (Courtesy of the Seiler estate.)

Carmon Phillips remembered, "Friday nights, we'd make a bunch of sandwiches to sell and load everything up. At daybreak, we'd build a big bonfire and set up the portable rope tow and the gasoline engine. We'd sell sandwiches to the skiers and charge a little bit for a 'lift ticket'—all the while working on the Forest Service to allow a ski area to be built on the mountain." (Courtesy of the late Carmon Phillips.)

On May 27, 1960, a 5-inch headline in the *Ruidoso News* proclaimed "Ruidoso gets $2 million ski resort." The first challenge was to build a 12-mile-long road up the mountain's steep slopes, a project estimated at $330,000. By 1965, the winding 12-mile road to the ski area was completely paved. The hexagonal buildings in the center of the photograph (designed to look like snowflakes from the air) were first used for lodging and later housed the children's ski school. Fourteen were planed, but only three were build. (Courtesy of the late Carmon Phillips.)

The Sierra Blanca Ski Area lodge was designed by Victor Lundry, named America's Outstanding Architect in 1958. Lundry was known for his unusual roofs; the pointed cones on the lodge's roof suggested a mountain range. Roy Parker, who managed the ski area from 1964 until 2004, remembered, "It took forever to get those darned points in the roof to quit leaking. That's an architect for you." (Courtesy of Roy Parker.)

In 1974, the national gasoline shortage prompted the $25 Ski Pak, which included meals, lodging, lift ticket, and ski rental. (Courtesy of the late Carmon Phillips.)

In 1962, a four-passenger gondola, built in Switzerland, was installed at the Sierra Blanca Ski Area. It was such a novelty in the 1960s that hundreds of people came to ride it during the summer and for moonlight rides in the winter. In 2009, it was still the only gondola operating in the state. (Both courtesy of the late Carmon Phillips.)

Skiers stand on a run called "The Face," at the top of the mountain facing the base of the ski area. On the other side of the peak, visitors have a view of the gypsum fields of White Sands National Monument in the distance. (Both courtesy of Roy Parker.)

Roy Parker came from Vail, Colorado, to take over management of the Sierra Blanca Ski Area in 1964. "The landscape changes so quickly, when I first came for the job interview, I thought it was a practical joke," Parker remembered. "I thought, 'No way is there a ski area in the middle of the desert.'" (Courtesy of Roy Parker.)

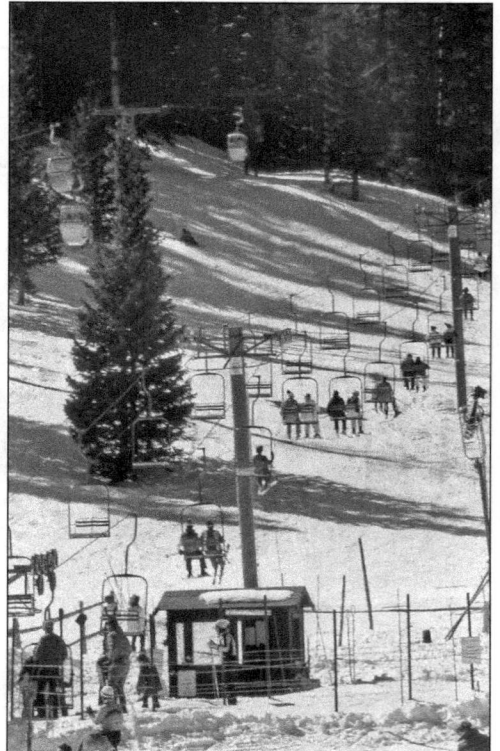

In 1965, the snow-making capacity was doubled and new trails like "Incredible" were opened. Chairlifts gradually replaced the earlier T-bars. (Courtesy of Roy Parker.)

In 1966, Apache Mountain Spirit Dancers performed a "snow dance" at the highest point of the ski area. The legend of the Mountain Spirits says that they saved injured Apache warriors whose companions were forced to leave them behind on the slopes of Sierra Blanca. The figure on the left is a clown. Artist Frederick Peso said "The clown is always the most powerful, even though he acts the fool." In the legend, the clown opens the cave where the warriors are hidden by touching the rock with a feather. (Both courtesy of Roy Parker.)

In 2009, Ski Apache had 11 chairlifts and 750 acres of skiable terrain. (Courtesy of Roy Parker.)

The giant figure in this 1963 photograph was reportedly made of wood and its surface packed with snow. It was reportedly burned at the end of the season. (Courtesy of the late Carmon Phillips.)

New Mexico's usually sunny skies prompt outdoor winter picnics. (Courtesy of Roy Parker.)

Quarter horse racing, in which horses sprint up to 440 yards, was a perfect fit for Ruidoso Downs. Owners and breeders from Texas and Oklahoma, many of whom made millions in the oil business, brought their adventurous "wildcat" spirit to the sport. (Courtesy of the late Carmon Phillips.)

# Seven

# AND THEY'RE OFF!

Sometime before 1910, Dr. S. M. Johnson came from Chicago and built the White Mountain Inn. Johnson, a very active and ambition Presbyterian minister, had a nervous breakdown and left the ministry for his health. He and his wife moved to Lincoln County and raise apples but found it difficult to get them to market. Johnson led efforts to improve roads first locally—hiring a crew and fixing the worst stretches himself—and then nationally. In 1915, an official delegation travelled from San Diego to Washington, D.C. They planned to go from El Paso to Roswell in one day, but reported that "soon after we started from El Paso . . . the conditions of the road did not admit of fast driving."

In 1924, the *El Paso Times* noted that G. A. Friedenbloom was in town petitioning the postal service to establish a mail route to a town he was creating. In 1926, he got his post office for what he named "Hollywood," after the Florida town of the same name. Unfortunately, there were 14 other "Hollywoods" in the United States, which caused some delays in mail delivery.

Dr. Johnson's son, H. V. ("Heck") Johnson, inherited land and water rights and began selling lots in 1933. He called his new development Palo Verde, but the postal service decided that there were too many towns with similar names, so in 1947, the name was changed to Green Tree.

Joetyne Wright lived in a log cabin with a dirt floor in what would become Ruidoso Downs. Her grandparents Fountain and Alice Miller owned land in the area. They also had a store and "traded with the Indians for baskets and beadwork," according to Wright.

The family owned a large tract of level land along the river that served as pasture for their cattle and a place for picnics and impromptu rodeos and horse races. The early races were usually between two horses and were run on a rough track whose finish line was 12 feet higher than the start. In 1945, the Ruidoso Ranch Hands Roundup was held at the arena, beginning with a parade that started at Montie's Riding Academy, some 5 miles away.

Crude improvements were made over the years, and the area opened as Hollywood Park in 1947. Gene Hensley bought the track in 1953 and changed its name to Ruidoso Downs. In 1958, residents of Green Tree voted overwhelmingly to change the town's name to Ruidoso Downs.

Hensley made improvements to the track and decided to concentrate on quarter horse racing, which at the time was much less lucrative than Thoroughbred racing. In 1956, several horsemen met in an Albuquerque bar and began bragging about their horses, many of which were mares carrying foals. They decided to race the as yet unborn foals in two years. The race, the All American Futurity, was run on Labor Day 1959 and was won by Huntley's Galobar for a purse of nearly $130,000. In 1978, the purse reached the $1 million mark, and it hit $2 million in 1982.

The Rainbow Futurity was added in 1964 and with the Ruidoso and All American Futurity forms the Triple Crown of quarter horse racing. As of 2007, the only horse to win all three races was Special Effort in 1981.

Lloyd Bennett (no relation to Clayton Bennett) operated a garage on Highway 70 in Hollywood. (Courtesy of Herb Brunell.)

The White Mountain Inn was originally built as a health sanatorium. It continued to operate as a lodging establishment when the photograph was taken in the 1940s. In 2008, it was a private residence. (Courtesy of Herb Brunell.)

With so many towns in the Southwest having names similar to Palo Verde, the U.S. Postal Service required that the name be changed to its English translation—Green Tree. (Courtesy of Herb Brunell.)

A number of sawmills operated in the area, harvesting the abundant timber in the nearby mountains. (Courtesy of the late Carmon Phillips.)

The flat pasture land along the river was used for steer roping and rodeos. (Courtesy of the late Carmon Phillips.)

The informal racing season lasted only a few weeks in the summer, so little effort was made to improve the facility. This photograph of a crude seating area and steward's stand was taken about 1948. The track was so uneven that horses had to run uphill on the home stretch. (Courtesy of Jackie McClanahan.)

Bill McCarty was 13 years old when he rode his horse, Martini, in a match race in 1945. He said, "Most of the early races were 'match races'—two horses running to see which one was fastest. I can't remember how much I won that day, but most races paid between $50 and $300." (Courtesy of Bill McCarty.)

Humor columnist George Noland wrote in the *Fort Worth Star-Telegram*, "Ruidoso, New Mexico, is the adult West Texan's Disneyland. Visiting Texans leave part of their money at the bars along the town's carnival-like main drag. They leave the rest of it at the race track." (Courtesy of Herb Brunell.)

The photograph here shows Gene Hensley (left), artist Peter Hurd, and cowboy singer Ray Reed (right). Reed began singing and performing in the 1930s, while working as a guide and entertainer in Yosemite Park. He joined the Cross-B Boys, and the band had their world premiere at the Navajo Lodge and became very popular. The band broke up in 1946, and Reed moved to Ruidoso with his family. He said, "I never did go for that fake stuff. I believe people like to see the real thing and hear the true Western songs, sung as they should be sung." He continued to perform, often offering trail rides and chuck wagon dinners. (Courtesy of Hubbard Museum of the American West.)

Bettors get a good look at the horses in the post parade just before the start of the race (above). The old sign is visible in the photograph of a quarter horse race (below). Both photographs were taken about 1960. (Both courtesy of the late Carmon Phillips.)

The horses in this photograph are Thoroughbreds rather than quarter horses. (Courtesy of the late Carmon Phillips.)

Races could be named for almost anything or anyone. In 1950, the fifth annual Central Bar and Grill Futurity was run. In the 1960s, races were often named for visiting celebrities. The photograph here of the Peter Hurd Handicap, held in 1969, shows Peter Hurd in the center. The horse Battle Bound won the race. (Courtesy of Dan Dee Cabins.)

The racing season gradually expanded to begin on Memorial Day weekend and end on Labor Day with the All American Futurity. (Courtesy of the late Carmon Phillips.)

R. D. and Joan Dale Hubbard purchased a controlling interest in the track in 1988. They invested $25 million to upgrade the facility during years when other racetracks were closing. In 1999, a casino was added to the track, and its revenue contributed to the race purses. The Hubbards have donated more than $23 million in grants to cultural and educational programs in Lincoln County and southeastern New Mexico. (Courtesy of the Hubbard Foundation.)

Mrs. Tod Browning taught school in a small cabin in the area that became known as Schoolhouse Park. Opal (left) and Della Wingfield were students. The small population of students made it difficult to maintain a school. Ruidoso's first public school opened in 1938. (Courtesy of the Wingfield family.)

# *Eight*

# Daily Life

Ruidoso has always been known as a resort town, and much of its economic and social life has been tied to tourism. An article in a 1936 *New Mexico Magazine* said, "Ruidoso before the middle of May is something of a ghost town. The dormant, sleepy little community almost overnight becomes a thriving, bustling city."

But Ruidoso is also a town with all the needs and challenges of any other—streets must be maintained, fires extinguished, children educated, medical emergencies met, and mail delivered.

In 1938, the town's first permanent school was built at the corner of Center and Wingfield Streets. Three years later, a gymnasium was built next to it for $5,000. (In 2008, the buildings housed the Ruidoso Municipal Court and the Ruidoso Athletic Club.) In 1946, Ruidoso High School opened. (The building later served as the middle school until 2008.) In 1982, Ruidoso High School opened on Warrior Drive.

In 1949, the telephone book consisted of two double-sided pages, and it included listings for Capitan and the U.S. Marine Hospital in Fort Stanton. Yolanda Pierson was the town's telephone operator. John Sigler, who worked for the electric company, said, "If there was a power outage and a couple people called, she'd call us and ask what the trouble was. Then she'd handle all the calls, and tell them, 'They're working on it, they should have it fixed in a couple hours.' " Bill McCarty remembered calling his parents from a navy ship in the Pacific: "She'd say, 'I know they're not home, but maybe they went to visit So-and-so.' She'd call all over town until she found them." One year, Yolanda and an old crank telephone rode in the Aspencade parade. In 1954, the first dial telephones came to Ruidoso. The 1955 telephone book contained detailed instructions for dialing the new phones as well as contacting another person on one's own party line.

The first street marker was installed in 1951 at the intersection of Main and Alto Roads, and in 1973, the first traffic light was installed in the same location, although the streets by then were named Sudderth and Mechem Drives. But Ruidosans have always had a casual attitude about street names. In 1951, a visitor remarked, "Visitors here for the first time can hardly find anyone they're looking for." In 1954, some 200 wooden street markers were installed, after first giving the streets some names. A letter to the editor in 1964 complained, "It would help some if the Ruidoso people knew the names of the streets. Why doesn't Ruidoso have sign posts, and house numbers?"

As more people came for the summer, businesspeople—many of them summer residents themselves—started providing them with the services they needed. The sign outside Brown's Café announces "Okies and Texans." (Courtesy of Mickey Cochran.)

The Covered Wagon Curios opened for business in the early 1930s and was still in business in the same location in 2009. (Courtesy of Mickey Cochran.)

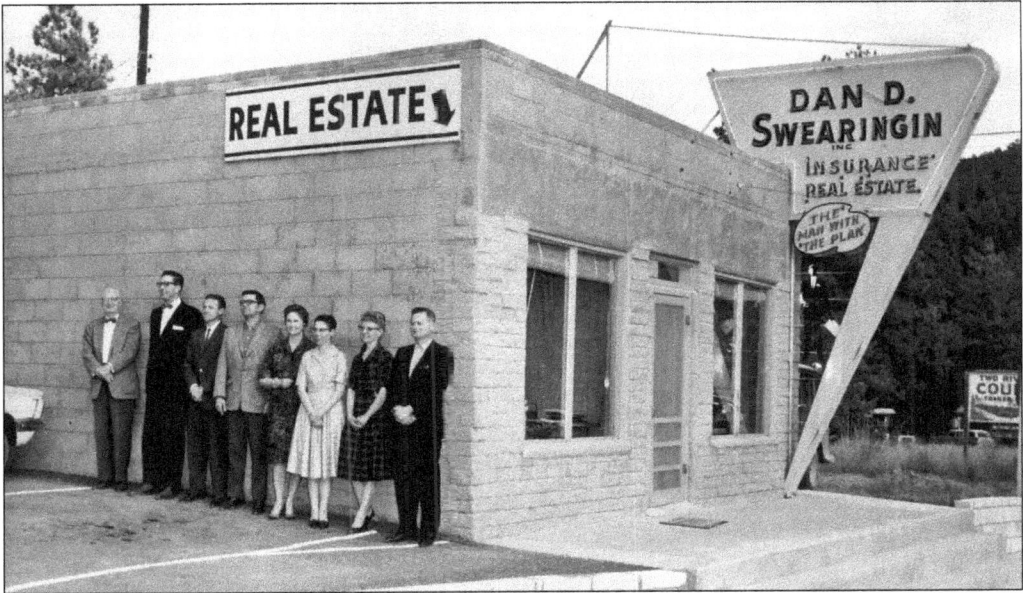

After spending his adolescence building and working at the Dan Dee Cabins, Dan D. Swearingin Jr. (second from left) went into the real estate and insurance business, advertising himself as "the man with a plan." Tommy Perteet is third from the left; Dave Parks is fourth from left. (Courtesy of the late Carmon Phillips.)

In 1946, Herbert Brunell Sr. opened Brunell's Dry Goods on Main Road. Brunell had operated a similar store in Alamogordo in 1935 and opened the Ruidoso store after spending summer vacations there. The store has been expanded and remodeled several times but was still owned and operated by the Brunell family in 2009. (Courtesy of Herb Brunell.)

Until the Ruidoso State Bank opened in 1953, the town had no bank. Bill McCarty, whose uncle owned several bars, remembered driving sacks of money to the bank in Alamogordo, his car weighed down by coins from the slot machines. (Courtesy of the late Carmon Phillips.)

In 1946, Dr. R. S. Sutton provided care for horse and automobile accidents as well as family medicine. His advertisement directed patients to his office "located in the center of the old golf course." The Ruidoso–Hondo Valley Hospital was built in the same area, on land donated by the White Mountain Development Company. The hospital opened in 1950 and was obliged to ask for donations of bedsheets, baby clothing, and dish towels. The ambulance was on loan from a Roswell funeral parlor. During the first busy summer season, the emergency room borrowed cots from Dan Dee Cabins. (Courtesy of the late Carmon Phillips.)

Ruidoso's first fire station and jail occupied the same building. Wayne Joyce, whose father, Coleman, served as a village police officer, remembered, "There was no jail, so criminals had to be driven to Carrizozo [40 miles away]. That would take all day, so by the time you got back, the rest of the miscreants would have shot up the whole town. After the jail was built, there was no way to feed the prisoners, so they arranged for the cafes on Main Road to feed them and send the town the bill. Dad would let them out of jail to eat breakfast and tell them, 'Now when you come back, you just go back in your cells and pull the doors shut' and they'd do it. Sometimes he'd let them out to walk up to see a movie at the Pueblo Theater." (Courtesy of Helen Barajas Woodfin.)

In 1947, all the town's firefighters were volunteers. In 1966, three paid firefighters were hired for $1.50 an hour. In the photograph are, from left to right, Wade Hedgecoke, Bert Weatherby, Wayne Estes, J. W. Peterson, John Ike Kennedy, Claude Peterson, Coke Hedgecoke, Elmo Vaughn, Joe Dryden, Ike Wingfield (mayor and fire chief), Dutch Collins, and unidentified. Dewey Gann is behind the fire truck. Frank Barajas and Jim Pickering are squatting with the dog, Ripper. (Courtesy of the Wingfield family.)

Pilot Ralph Brown's newspaper advertisement in 1953 said, "When you need to make a hurried trip, contact Ralph Brown, pilot." His company also offered emergency medical transport by air. (Courtesy of Herb Brunell.)

In 1950, Bill McCarty's family business, White Mountain Development Company, donated 153 acres to the village for an airport. A column in the *Ruidoso News*, "Airport Activities," reported the comings and goings of the many private pilots and airplanes. McCarty remembered, "Another fellow and I were standing by the runway, and we heard a pilot radio that he'd be coming in for a landing, and to have his rental car ready. About 10 seconds later, the plane landed, swerved all over the runway, and went into the ditch. The passengers were trying to climb out, and the guy jumped out and shouted, 'Where's my rent car? I've got a horse running in the eighth race!'" (Courtesy of Herb Brunell.)

Seventeen fatal airplane crashes occurred between 1965 and 1985, including one in 1982 in which three men died when their plane crashed near Sudderth Drive. A report in 1980 said, "The existing airport is considered one of the most dangerous in New Mexico because of steep terrain, the short runway, and the proximity to existing residential development." Bill McCarty, himself a pilot, maintained that the accidents were "mostly pilot error." Mechem Drive crosses at the top of the photograph. A new airport on Fort Stanton Mesa opened in 1987. (Courtesy of the late Carmon Phillips.)

The tow truck from the Midway Garage is caught in the 1941 flood. (Courtesy of Jeri Hurley.)

# Nine

# DISASTERS

Floods and fires are a threat in Ruidoso's forested mountain location. The town is built along a narrow canyon at the foot of a huge mountain. Rain and snow melt all funnel into one small river.

Dave Parks remembered a damaging flood in 1941, when he was eight years old. "Both Upper Canyon bridges were washed out and the river cut a new channel and got blocked by a pile of debris. It turned a corner and hit a cabin and that cabin just exploded, that's the only way I can describe it, and there was a cast iron cookstove and an iron bed frame floating on the water. Don't ask me to explain that, but I remember it clearly."

Forty-three cabins were washed away in the flood. Most of the town's bridges were washed out, and trees were dropped to make temporary bridges. E. C. Triebe (who owned movie theaters in Ruidoso and Roswell), Peter Espinosa, and Manuel Chaney drowned when their car was washed off a bridge near Tinnie.

In 1965, flooding caused $120 million in damage from Ruidoso to Riverside, 30 miles down the Hondo Valley. In 1984, the Rio Ruidoso flooded again, with water 3 feet above the river's banks. In July 2008, flooding washed out 13 bridges and left Upper Canyon residents stranded for weeks.

But fire is the real threat in Ruidoso. Winters with little snowfall lead to dry windy springs that make the forests a tinderbox ready for a careless person or a bolt of lightning to ignite.

The U.S. Forest Service predicted that 1950 would be "the Southwest's worst fire year." That summer, a fire burned in the Capitan Mountains north of Ruidoso. A small black bear cub was found clinging to a burned tree. The rescued cub was named "Smokey" after the cartoon character designed for a campaign for fire prevention.

Snow, wind, fire, or flood—Ruidoso residents and visitors take it in stride. As Bill McCarty noted, "There hasn't been a disaster yet that slowed down Ruidoso."

Wayne Joyce remembered, "In 1941, it rained all through June, July, August and September. It was the rainiest, mussiest summer we ever had. The bridge over Carrizo Creek on the road into Ruidoso got washed out and people couldn't get up here, and they couldn't leave. Some men felled a pine tree across the creek and people could walk across that, but it was quite a while before the water got down and the bridge was rebuilt." The photographs show Two Rivers Park (above) and Upper Canyon (below). (Above courtesy of Herb Brunell; below courtesy of Dave Parks.)

Residents along the Rio Ruidoso awoke on July 27, 2008, to a roar of rushing water. Fourteen inches of rain had fallen in the previous 24 hours, and the enormous drainage area brought all the water to one small river. Thirteen bridges were washed out and 350 homes damaged or destroyed. Nearly 600 people were rescued by ladder, rope tether, and helicopter, and 200 Upper Canyon residents were stranded for several days. The river, 20 times its normal size, destroyed the electronic tote board at the Ruidoso Downs Race Track. (Both courtesy of Herb Brunell.)

In 1953, a fire started about noon in the attic of the Central Bar and Grill and was out of control in a few seconds. In three hours, the Central, the Mint Bar, and Star Liquors were all destroyed. Several of the damaged buildings had only been recently renovated. Hundreds of residents and visitors helped the many volunteer fire companies that responded. The fire was stopped by the Ruidoso Bar's two-story stone wall. Windows in buildings across the street were broken by the heat. (Both courtesy of Herb Brunell.)

Dixie Sigler remembered, "When the fire happened, I was working in the Spanish Nook Café, which was up the street on the opposite side. My uncle, who was a preacher came in, while half the town was across the street fighting the fire, and started yelling about how it was a judgment because of all the drinking and gambling that went on in there. The rest of the customers were staring at him, and I just pretended that I didn't know him." (Both courtesy of Herb Brunell.)

The Lookout Tower was built in 1940 for fire protection by the U.S. Forest Service. In 1945, fire danger was so high that tower watchers were on duty for 48 days straight. That same year, local residents, including watchers at the two fire towers, saw a huge explosion in the western sky—the test of the first atomic bomb at nearby White Sands Proving Ground. The tower still stood on a ridge overlooking Midtown in 2009. (Courtesy of Helen Montgomery.)

Ruidoso continues to owe its safety to the many firefighters who respond to wildland fires, including the Mescalero Hot Shots. (Courtesy of the Smokey Bear Historic Park.)

The injured bear cub was cared for by Ray Bell of the New Mexico Department of Game and Fish, whose daughter, Judy, poses with Smokey in the photograph below. Smokey was three to four months old and weighed about 5 pounds. The *Ruidoso News* reported, " 'Smokey' or 'Hotfoot Teddy' as he is sometimes called, had all four feet badly burned in the fire. The tiny injured bear, playing in a cardboard box in the Department of Game and Fish office in Santa Fe, speaks more eloquently than any poster the need to 'Prevent Forest Fires.' " (Courtesy of the Smokey Bear Historic Park.)

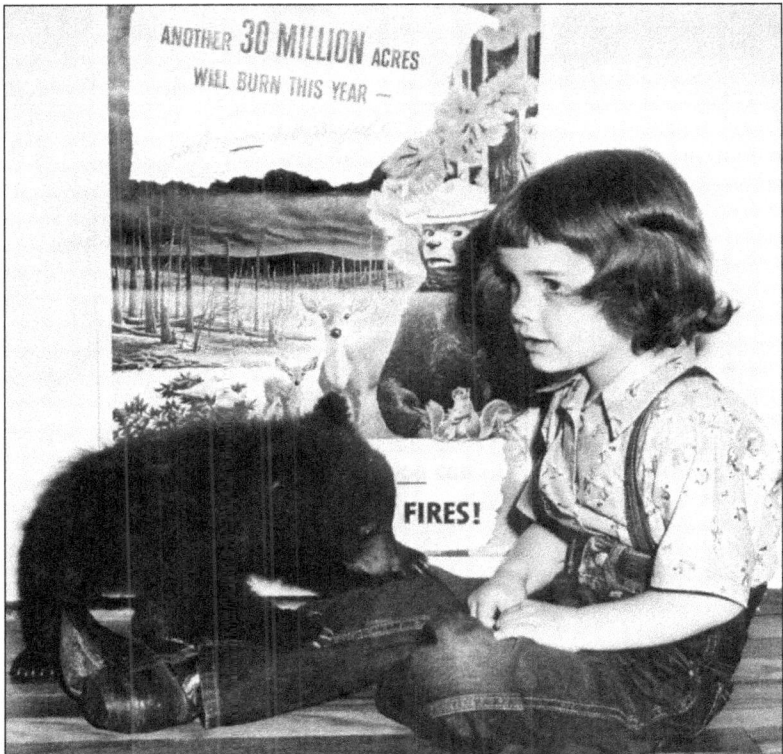

After his recovery, Smokey was flown to the National Zoo in Washington, D.C. When he died in 1976, he was returned to Capitan. His grave is in Smokey Bear Historic Park. (Courtesy of the Smokey Bear Historic Park.)

Betsy Seiler, whose parents built a cabin in Ruidoso in 1944, takes a ride in a burro cart. "My parents loved to ride," she said, "so we always had horses and ponies that we rented from the stables." (Courtesy of the Seiler estate.)

# Ten

# DISCOVER RUIDOSO

Since its earliest days, Ruidoso has been in a constant state of discovery. In 1975, the *El Paso Herald-Post* noted that "you don't refer to Ruidoso as a 'sleepy little village' anymore." Newspaper and magazine articles of every decade warn that the "little town in the mountains" is a secret no longer. And the town has certainly grown; during the 1990s, Lincoln County's population grew 59 percent. A larger portion of the population lives there all year. Festivals and other events bring visitors almost every weekend of the year.

But the essentials remain the same. Ruidoso is an island of scenic mountain beauty and—even in an age of air-conditioning—continues to attract those who want to escape a desert summer. Pleasures remain simple—a picnic or walk in the woods, a horseback ride, or a stroll along the shops of Midtown. Those looking for gambling or nightlife can still find it in the town's modest casinos and taverns. Family cabins are filled with several generations, each amusing themselves in their own way, all of them enjoying their time together.

And they may echo the words of the *El Paso Times* reporter who wrote in 1889, "All who have been there agree that it is the most beautiful country they ever saw."

The Flying J Wranglers opened the Flying J Ranch north of Ruidoso in 1982, providing chuck wagon suppers and Western stage shows. In this photograph, from left to right, are Randy Jones, Corinne Ripple, Roy Black, Cindy Hobbs, and James Hobbs. (Courtesy of the Flying J Wranglers.)

Sculptor Dave McGary's "Free Spirits at Noisy Water" (above) was installed in front of the Museum of the Horse in 1995. R. D. and Joan Dale Hubbard created the museum in 1992 to house an enormous collection of horse-related materials, like saddles, stirrups, wagons, and carriages donated by avid horsewoman Anne C. Stradling. In 1999, it became the Hubbard Museum of the American West. (Courtesy of the Hubbard Museum of the American West.)

The photograph shows the finish of the 2008 All American Futurity at Ruidoso Downs Race Track. Stolis Winner (right) beat Jet Black Patriot by half a length. In 2009, Stolis Winner was disqualified when random drug testing revealed caffeine. Jet Black Patriot was declared the winner. (Courtesy of Ruidoso Downs Race Track.)

The first Cowboy Symposium, founded by musician Ray Reed, took place in 1989. The three-day October event draws fans of old-time music and chuck wagon cooking, with teams competing to produce the best biscuits, beef, beans, and fruit cobbler in 24 hours. (Courtesy of Frederic Moras.)

The Spencer Theater was built by wealthy arts patron Jackie Spencer. Architect Antoine Predock designed the state-of-the-art theater, which opened in 1997. (Courtesy of Brad Cooper.)

The Inn of the Mountain Gods is a luxury resort owned by the Mescalero Apache tribe. The resort offers golf, horseback riding, live concerts, and a casino. The inn is built on one side of Mescalero Lake, with a stunning view of Sierra Blanca. (Courtesy of Harvey Foster.)

# BIBLIOGRAPHY

Coe, George. *Frontier Fighter*. Chicago: R. R. Donnelley and Sons, 1984.

Coe, Louise. *The Lady and the Law Books*. Albuquerque: Modern Press, 1981.

Coe, Wilbur. *Ranch on the Ruidoso: The Story of a Pioneer Family in New Mexico, 1871–1968*. New York: Alfred A. Knopf, 1971.

Lincoln County Postmasters. *History of Lincoln County Post Offices*. Ruidoso, NM: *Ruidoso News*, 1962.

Mangan, Frank. *Ruidoso Country*. El Paso, TX: Mangan Books, 1994.

NewspaperArchive.com

*Ruidoso News*, various issues.

Seckler, Herb. *Ruidoso Countryside: The Early Days*. Ruidoso, NM: self-published, 1987.

———. *Hoofnotes from the Downs*. Ruidoso, NM: self-published, 1990.

Sonnichsen, C. L. *The Mescalero Apaches*. Norman, OK: University of Oklahoma Press, 1958.

Traylor, Herbert L. *Tales of the Sierra Blanca*. Roswell, NM: Pioneer Printing, 1983.

Traylor, Herbert L. and Louise Coe Runnels. *The Saga of the Sierra Blanca*. Roswell, NM: Old-Time Publications, 1986.

WPA Writer's Project. *Old Lincoln County Pioneer Stories*. Lincoln, NM: Lincoln County Historical Society Publications, 1994.

www.ingramcontent.com/pod-product-compliance
Lightning Source LLC
Chambersburg PA
CBHW050547110426
42813CB00008B/2283